Getting there

SIGNS TO GUIDE YOU ALONG THE
BROKEN ROAD TO LIFE-CHANGING HOPE

LINETTE BUMFORD

Unless otherwise identified, all Scripture quotations in this publication are taken from the Holy Bible, New International Version® (NIV®). Copyright © 1973, 1978, 1984, 2011 by Biblica, Inc®. Used by permission of Zondervan. All rights reserved.

Verses marked (NKJV) are taken from the New King James Version. Copyright © 1982 by Thomas Nelson, Inc. Used by permission. All rights reserved.

Verses marked (NLT) are taken from the Holy Bible, New Living Translation. Copyright © 1996, 2004, 2007 by Tyndale House Foundation. Used by permission of Tyndale House Publishers, Inc., Carol Stream, Illinois 60188. All rights reserved.

Verses marked (TLB) are taken from the The Living Bible copyright © 1971 by Tyndale House Foundation. Used by permission of Tyndale House Publishers Inc., Carol Stream, Illinois 60188. All rights reserved.

Copyright © 2018 by Linette Bumford

Loved (5.5x8.5) Self-Publishing Template © 2017 Renee Fisher
https://www.reneefisher.com

Cover Design: Ryan «ryanurz» Biore
Interior formatting and design: Nelly Murariu at PixBeeDesign.com

Cover Photo: © Adobe Stock
Author Photo: Kerry Paradis

ISBN-13: 978-1-7323410-0-5
ISBN-10: 1-7323410-0-1

"I didn't realize just how many road signs there were until I read *Getting There* by Linette Bumford. It brought me hope to know that I am not the only one traveling on the "*Winding Road Ahead*," accidentally (or purposely) taking a "*Dead End*" road, while giving myself permission to make a "*U-Turn*." Linette's book inspires hope to those traveling the broken road while learning how to "*Merge/Yield*," slow down for a "*Detour*," and stop to "*R.E.S.T.*" well."

—RENEE FISHER
Author of *Forgiving Others, Forgiving Me* and many other books

"Linette Bumford has creatively captured the essence of our life journey from pain to healing. She takes you on the ride of your life as you travel down every imaginable road with all of its twists and turns that try to confuse and frustrate you from reaching the destination of hope and healing. Her transparency as she shares her own story will encourage you that even in pain God has a plan for your life. His plan is far better that our plan and the only thing that stands in the way is fear and doubt. I encourage you to climb aboard, fasten your seat belt and fix your own rear view mirror and allow God to navigate you through your own personal challenges."

—REV. MICHELE AMODIO
Founder of House of Refuge Ministry

"Linette has discovered the freedom that belongs to those who step into the light of God's love, vulnerably facing things we would rather forget. Opening herself up to examine the difficulties and triumphs along her path, she simultaneously invites the reader to join her in self-reflection, meditation on Scripture, and living into the fullness of God's grace. *Getting There* is a powerful book to use in personal reflection or with a group of women wanting to deepen their faith and their friendships."

—ANDREA WENBURG
Voice of Influence podcast host
Author of *UNFROZEN: Stop Holding Back and Release the Real You*
www.voiceofinfluence.net

Dedication
To Nacelle

On my own I traveled the Outlets of No
That brought me to choices to make, forward to Go!
I pray you find courage to let go of the wheel,
To find hope in the Lord when your heart needs to heal.
My Mack truck U-Turn freed me of a ton.
Wrong Ways and Dead Ends, I pray you have none.
Unexpected and exciting places life will take you.
May my roadmap help make your twists and turns few,
But, if you must, may you be blessed with Guardrails
And have courage and strength to tell of your tale.
Should you find yourself off the path and winding astray,
Look for the signs that point to God's Only Way.
The roads have been rough, and unexpected, too,
But I'd travel again, knowing now that it brought me to you.

Contents

Letter to the Reader   1
Foreword   3

Introduction – Roadside Assistance   5

Mile Marker 1: Enter   13
Mile Marker 2: No Outlet   31
Mile Marker 3: Winding Road Ahead   45
Mile Marker 4: Wrong Way – Do Not Enter   57

Rest Area 1: R.E.S.T.   75

Mile Marker 5: Dead End   81
Mile Marker 6: U-Turn   97
Mile Marker 7: One Way   111
Mile Marker 8: Road Work Ahead   123

Rest Area 2: A.R.E.A.   139

Mile Marker 9: No Passing Zone   145
Mile Marker 10: Merge/Yield   159
Mile Marker 11: Detour   175
Mile Marker 12: Exit   187

Road-trip Remix (Songs and Psalms for Getting There)   199
Notes – Billboards   201
Acknowledgments – Bumper Stickers   205
About the Author   210

Letter to the Reader

One day while I was driving home, tears began to fall from my eyes, and then laughter came from my belly. I thought, *How am I laughing and crying at the same time? I must be losing my mind.* But as the fog of my emotions began to lift, I could see in my mind's eye visions of YOU—an abandoned woman, a broken child, a mistress, an addict, a loner, a lonely single, an ex-wife, a masked churchgoer, a double-lifer, fear-ridden, a hole-filler. I could see all who are exhausted, confused, sad, and hopeless…all who wouldn't dare tell a soul that they feel one or more of those struggles!

Do you have a hard time looking someone in the eye? Do you feel they will see your past and your secret sins? I know it was like that for me. It took me years to come out of hiding and take off the mask that I had worn for so long. I came to a point in my life where I was willing to face my past but not allow it to define me any longer!

Though I'm a serious *introvert,* God continues to put me in situations and opportunities that require me to be really "out there!" The message in this book is about *what a changed life looks like.* Some changes can be drastic. Some are slow and steady. Some are painful, making you shake your head and sometimes even shake your fist! But regardless of how the change occurs, please know that change is *so worth it!*

Take that proverbial first step on your journey, and while you process your mess, may you allow God to use you right where you are—on the road less traveled. Come along as we navigate the road signs along the broken road to life-changing hope. My prayer is that you will begin to see your past differently, with a fresh perspective, as you traverse your road and navigate the everyday path necessary for *Getting There*!

Linette Bumford

Author & Life Coach

Foreword

I was at a crossroads when I met Linette in the Rise Up Writers Facebook group led by Jolene Underwood.

I could see where I wanted to go with the direction of my life and business—but I needed help "getting there."

Just by being herself, Linette offered me friendship as well as her refreshing wisdom that comes from traveling a broken road herself. It's easy to learn from Linette because she is a humble guide with a teachable spirit.

Linette is a reservoir of knowledge that runs deep. I had no idea just how much I would need her help in the last year—and I was *her* Life Coach! Not only did Linette become the teacher, but she also became my guide to finding hope and life change along the broken road of life.

It's easy to learn from Linette.

That's why I believe *Getting There* will help many others—like me—who are trying to get from point A to point B.

Maybe you're struggling with a toxic relationship and feeling like you're at a *"Dead End."* Maybe your business is fledgling, and you don't know how to make a *"U-Turn."* Maybe you feel so hurt by God that you want off His *"One Way"* street.

Friends, I hope you'll give this book *and* Linette a chance to sit down and talk with you like a friend. This is a judgment-free *"No Passing Zone!"*

It's okay; Linette is a safe person who can be trusted to lead you around those many *"Winding Roads Ahead"* as well as those unexpected and painful *"Detours."*

Soon, like me, you'll be seeing signs EVERYWHERE! Instead of being afraid, you'll welcome them as a challenge for growth, hope, and life change!

Are you feeling stuck?

Do you need a little push "getting there?"

What are you waiting for? Release that parking brake, and let's get going! Roll those windows down, open the book, and let Linette in your life. I know her story will inspire you as it did me.

Linette's questions at the end of each Mile Marker will help you truly process your own hurts and hang-ups. She'll help you drive your car all the way home to *"Exit"* and (*gasp!*) teach you how to *"R.E..S.T.!"*

Linette is the kind of a person who gives herself freely, one who you can't help but welcome into your life. Do you need courage and transparency to chase your dreams? Then let's all "get there" together!

Your Dream Defender,

Renee Fisher

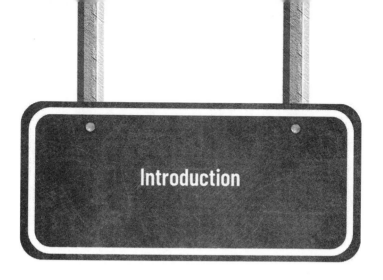

Introduction

Roadside Assistance

*"Most people have a highway to upset and a
dirt road to happiness."* *(Tony Robbins)*

I'm sure you've heard it said that "Life is a journey," and
like most journeys, it's never fun to travel alone! After
all, the Lord God did say, *"It's not good for man to be alone.
I will make a helper suitable for him"* (Genesis 2:18).

Although this verse is referring to the special relationship of
marriage between a man and woman (which we will definitely
get to later on in the book), I do believe we are not meant to
travel life alone. We need one another. What would life be like if
we didn't have family and good friends to confide in and share
our feelings and experiences with? That's why I decided to write
this book, so we can travel together and spend some quality time
getting to know one another while experiencing all the mishaps,
joys, and adventure that life has to offer. After all, life's journey

is not only about our final destination (for which there are really only two options), but also about the experiences along the way!

Like every road trip, you need to head out prepared in order to get to your destination. Years ago, the most important thing to bring on a road trip was AAA roadmap and travel plan. Today, that is so obsolete. Now we totally rely on our trustworthy GPS to get us from point A to point B. Unfortunately, our GPS sometimes has a mind of its own, taking us through back roads that don't make any sense, and ultimately guiding us to the wrong place. There's just something about that voice talking to us from our GPS that we feel we must follow, even when we know it's taking us the wrong way. When we do muster up enough courage not to follow its instructions, we hear that infamous, "Recalculating!"

Our GPS gives us some choices to make so that we feel like we are in control, but really, we are at its mercy. We can choose the fastest route, the route using more highways, the shortest route, or the most direct route. Then, after making our selection, we frequently ask, "Why is it taking me this way?" That is kind of how life is. We are given certain choices to make, but the outcome often brings us to a similar question, "Why is this happening to me?"

On our journey, road signs all along the way are really warning signs meant to protect us. Signs like:

Most of us adhere to those signs, knowing if we don't, it would cause us harm. But then there are signs like:

We sometimes consider these signs optional and choose to ignore them. Isn't that so true in life? Our loving Savior gives us signs to protect us, but we consider some of them optional and choose to ignore them, only to have to deal with the consequences. Isaiah 7:14 says,

> *"Therefore the Lord will himself will give you a sign: The virgin will conceive and give birth to a son, and will call him Immanuel."*

The intention of *Getting There* is to provide some insight from my own experiences that might prove helpful to you if you have lost your direction, have a flat tire on the side of the road and are temporarily stuck, or have run out of gas and feel stranded. There's nothing more exhilarating than when someone pulls up next to you and offers to point you in the right direction, or helps change your flat tire, or even tows you to the filling station so you can get refueled to continue your journey. Wherever you may find yourself in this journey called *life*, let's do it together so we can experience the joy of the journey and allow "God who works in you to will and to act in order to fulfill his good purpose" (Philippians 2:13).

I've had so many detours in my life journey that I found myself always questioning if God had good intentions for me. One day, God graciously gave me an answer to release me from a paralytic state in my faith journey. I was paralyzed by the question that haunts so many people:

Why, God? Why have you let certain things happen in my life?

This is one of the most asked and most crippling questions in a believer's life. One day, I was reminded of what the Apostle Paul said in 2 Corinthians 1:3-4,

> *"Praise be to the God and Father of our Lord Jesus Christ, the Father of compassion and the God of all comfort, who comforts us in all our troubles, so that we can comfort those in any trouble with the comfort we ourselves receive from God."*

I realized in that moment that God was calling me to the ministry of comfort. I might not have all the answers, but I have experienced the compassion and comfort of God in my own journey, and hopefully it can bring some clarity to the confusion that accompanies that "why" question in your life.

Pain can make you feel broken and of no value. Over time, that pain can really take root and cause an internal dying that we try to manage through external manifestations. You become angry and short-fused, or you begin to use other therapies (drinking, eating, shopping, sex, drugs, etc.) to create an outlet, surface relief. You question what kind of person you've become. Who could love someone who has done X or thinks Y? Your relationships are superficial.

I felt that way for a long time. It took me years to understand why, and then I realized it was because I knew it was a façade. I wasn't who people thought I was. Of course, this wasn't intentional. It had become my survival mechanism. I rejected their care and love and wanted to maintain control of what got in and what stayed out of my heart. No one else was going to have control over my heart! Except I finally came to realize that I didn't even have control over my own heart. That's when I decided to give the control over to God.

I welcome you to travel with me through stories of my own experiences and the amazing *power* that comes from knowing and trusting Jesus Christ with *all of it*! God's light shines in the dark for all who need just enough light for the next step in life's journey. To discover that light, I had to go through a process, a journey, of moving through where I was to where I wanted to be and, in some cases, accepting where God put me, rather than where I was trying to go.

Come along as we navigate life with unstoppable perseverance by allowing the road signs along the way to guide us to our desired destination. Let's exchange that old outdated GPS for the Word of God that is a light unto our path and for the divine leading of the Holy Spirit.

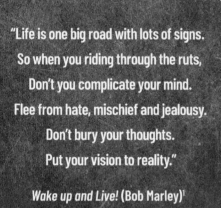

"Life is one big road with lots of signs.
So when you riding through the ruts,
Don't you complicate your mind.
Flee from hate, mischief and jealousy.
Don't bury your thoughts.
Put your vision to reality."

Wake up and Live! (Bob Marley)[1]

MILE
MARKER

1

Enter

*The invitation to a life of
hope along the broken road.*

he unknown. We see an *"Enter"* sign, but we don't know
what is around the corner. Sometimes we can see where
it's taking us. Other times, we only see the invitation.
We either have the courage to go for it, or we hesitate and pass
it up. In some cases, we are taken into circumstances we don't
ask for. But we enter and have to find our own way out, hurt,
confused, abandoned, like a pawn, with lack of purpose, floundering,
pulled in multiple directions. Absorbing what is going on. Taking
it all in. Observing, but taking no action. We do what we're told
and wrestle with the emotions.

As children, our view of the world is not skewed by experience
as much as it is in our adult life. Life invites us to experience it.
Sometimes our experiences happen by our own choice, while
other experiences happen *to* us. At some point in our life, we
recognize that we are on a road. It truly is the road less traveled,
because it's yours. Only *you* will have this path. People will come

alongside your path, and some will even merge on and off, but the path is yours alone. The beauty of it is you don't have to *be* alone. Let your soul accept the invitation of enlightenment, love, and being known. You will experience things that will hurt you. You'll feel confused, abandoned, and used. You'll feel at times that you lack purpose, like you're floundering about with no sense of understanding, and as if life is playing a cruel joke with you as the punch line. You'll be pulled in multiple directions, with a lack of confidence. And sometimes you'll just sit back and take it all in. Just like when you're in the backseat on a road trip—not the driver, not the navigator, just a spectator watching the world pass by. You'll take in the scenery and dream. This is what life offers us: opportunities to experience. With experience comes the bountiful fruit of wisdom. So, I invite you to begin this road trip. Join this ride.

As we journey together, my prayer is that you will know you are not alone. I extend the same invitation that Jesus has extended. Come. Just as you are. Isn't it a great feeling when we are invited to an event? Whether it's a party, dinner, or coffee, when someone thinks of us and wants to be in our presence, their invitation makes us feel loved and known. It's an amazing feeling to be considered and invited. And what a heartbreak when we aren't included and wanted to be. Have you ever not been invited to something, struggled with that feeling of being left out… forgotten? The path to Jesus is an invitation to no longer be forgotten or depend on others to make you feel included. Jesus offers us an infinite invitation that no person can provide. We are off to great place in this adventure of a life with Jesus.

I would not change a single thing about my past. As you read through the next 12 chapters of highlights from my own experiences, please know this. I would not change it. In the moments, I thought differently. I begged a different prayer. But, because *you* are holding these words and relating to this, I feel honored that the Lord would answer my prayer, "Use *me*. Change *me*."

The path to Jesus is an invitation to no longer be forgotten or depend on others to make you feel included.

Some of the stories are not stories I am proud to tell, but I am proud that the Lord can be glorified through them. It's an honor to feel that these words you are reading are reaching you because He wants them to. There are times when I close my eyes and think about the time before I entered this life on earth. I imagine God creating my character, forming me into who I am, ready for His calling. It reminds me of those Build-a-Bear Workshops. I imagine Him designing every aspect of my physical being, the hair on my head, my skin, my eyes. Then He designed what I would be. He breathed this calling into my heart. I imagine He spoke these words, "You, my daughter, will be strong. You will be courageous. You will bear hardship. You will be ridiculed. You will be alone. You will make choices that I will not like, but I love you. You will find Me, and together we will fulfill your calling. I will make a way for you. I will make a way for you to find Me."

He has also breathed into you. He created you to fulfill a great purpose. If you have not already begun a relationship with Him, I hope that this book, these words, are a way for Him to find you and awaken the heart He spoke to before your life even began. Can you hear it? Can you hear Him say, "I love you! I made you. I welcome you"?

There are countless stories of how God was glorified through some of the hardest of circumstances. I encourage you to study Matthew chapter 1. For many years, I blew right past this long list of names in Jesus' lineage. However, it has the most important of references. It is the very beginning of the New Testament, the "entry" into fully understanding purpose in pain, wisdom from story, and how God intended to use everyone and everything for His glory. Everything led to the birth of Jesus Christ, the birth of redemption.

But, don't miss it. Some of these people had to go through difficult things—adultery, murder, prostitution, child bearing out of wedlock, just to name a few. Matthew 1 only touches on Jesus' lineage, but each person mentioned bears a story. A story with purpose that leads to a road of the greatest of stories: Jesus' birth and the birth of redemption for us all.

There is power in our stories. And just as those stories in Jesus' lineage have served a purpose for us, *our* stories also serve a purpose. God wants to use your story, and my story, for His glory. You would think that I would just let God heal me and move on. Why "expose" myself like this? But just moving on would be pride, which keeps me from sharing the grandeur of who God is and what a relationship with Jesus can do for your life.

I invite you to "*Enter*" this ride with me and with yourself. There will be questions in every chapter to guide you along the way. I welcome you to write your roadmap, look through your rearview mirror, and allow Jesus to navigate your heart.

There is power in our stories.

I really think Dr. Seuss was on to something in *Oh, The Places You'll Go!* Life will take us to some *great* places, but we will also traverse some challenging and difficult roads. I'm sure you will agree that our past is made up of good and bad times that shape and mold our perspective. No matter how old we are, little bits of residue from our past cling to our "windshield," obstructing our view. Thankfully, with God's help, our view can be made clean and clear as we learn from our past and leave it behind in a healthy way. That is my prayer for each of us as we travel together. We all have heard, "Leave your past in the past," and "Don't look in the rearview mirror. Your future is in front of you." Yes, we can leave our past in the past, but if we don't leave it there in a healthy way and view it the way God does, then we lose. We lose out on mounds of riches, in the currency of wisdom. Because, as we've also all heard, "You don't know where you're going, unless you know where you've been." Your past is a roadmap to your future. That is not to say that your past has to repeat itself. Quite the opposite. With the guidance of the Holy Spirit, you can create a life full of purpose and abundance.

Road trips are always adventurous because we never really know what to expect from our starting point to the final destination. There will always be traffic jams, detours, and wrong turns along the way. There will be times when we will need to make legal and illegal U-turns in order to get back on the right road. Many times, circumstances and experiences we go through end up being a lot longer than we anticipated, but the key is to find the joy, wisdom, and beauty in where you are.

Life, like every vehicle, provides us with rearview mirrors for our protection, and it is important to glance back every now and then. But in order to progress, we need to focus on what lies ahead, staying alert and cautious, aware of our surroundings and anticipating any sudden mishaps that could occur. In our present age of technology, our vehicles are equipped with safety alerts that warn us when we swerve over the line into another lane, as well as automatic braking that slows our car when we're distracted and about to collide into someone or something. I sometimes wonder if this new technology is really helpful or if it just allows us to be *more* distracted rather than less. Regardless, we still need to use one of the most important pieces of protection— our seat belts. I recently flew on a new plane, and the flight attendant was joking about the many advanced technologies and the extravagant costs of the new plane. Yet the seat belt hasn't changed in more than fifty years. According to the flight attendant, it's the same old seat belt from a 1957 Chevy. God's Word is like that 1957 Chevy seat belt. It doesn't need to change. It's safe just the way it was made and intended. The world around us may change and advance, but His Word is safe for whatever we face. On our road trip, it's vitally important to remember to buckle up for safety!

Looking In My Rearview Mirror

I think it's fair to say that we all come from some measure of dysfunction in our family, although some dysfunctions are clearly more debilitating than others. I can truly say that my childhood family life was unusual. My parents got married to and divorced from *each other* three times. Yes, you read that correctly—three times. I guess they thought the third time was the charm.

Divorce is never easy for any child, but going through it three times definitely made a unique impact on me (and, of course, my siblings). Like most divorce scenarios, my parents fought a lot. Their first divorce is somewhat of a blur for me. I was too young to really process what was going on with them, but the one thing that really affected me was seeing my father every other weekend. Since my mother didn't want him to know where we were living, we would always meet at some remote location to make the exchange of kids. This put a lot of pressure on me as a five-year-old child, because I was the middle person who set up meetings between my parents. I remember one time when my father manipulated me into telling him where we lived by saying that Santa Claus wouldn't be able to find us. So, I spilled the beans. My mother was very angry that I divulged our address. I felt responsible for not being able to keep "our little secret" from my father. Being in the middle of my parents and trying to please both of them was a heavy burden at such a young age. But it turned out that letting my father know our address proved to be a good thing, because eventually they got back together again and remarried on New Year's Eve.

At the time, we were living in California, but since my father was in active duty in the military, it was not unusual for us to move around a lot. Not long after we were back together as a family, he was reassigned to Tennessee, where he bought a house. For the time being, things were pretty good. My father had a history of being a heavy drinker, which caused a lot of problems, but he seemed to stop drinking, to the relief of all of us. I also believe this was a big reason that things were going better between my parents.

As a child, going through this type of back and forth was confusing. I remember times of thinking I had been forgotten. Why wasn't I important enough to be considered in this process? I was too young at the time to think anything complex about my parents, but later in life I remember thinking about how selfish they were. They only thought of themselves. If they had broken up and led better lives separately for our overall well-being, that *may* have helped. But whether they were together or apart, it was hurtful. I felt used, like a pawn in a chess game. I had no choice but to take it all in, and I did just that. I observed, and I prayed. Looking back, I would call it a cry out for relief. The prayers to understand why would come later. But let's be real, when you're going through that hard thing, all you want is for it to go away or for something else to come and take you away from the hurt. I prayed for relief and peace. Over and over, I prayed, and I cried. And God answered that prayer. He provided the church. He gave me a way. He provided just as He said He would. He showed me early on and over and over again. He shone His headlights on my dark path and provided hope in these circumstances. The church became my refuge, and at the age of five, I first gave my life to Jesus.

Caution – Bump In the Road

During one of the times my parents were together, my father was deployed during Desert Storm. His absence started to affect my mother. She became depressed and started going out a lot, shopping and spending money we didn't have, doing whatever it took to help her cope. When my father returned home, things were not the same. I should say, he wasn't the same. I was always very close to my father, but something changed him during his time in Desert Storm. He had become very controlling and somewhat militant. The dad I knew and loved had become hard and uncaring. He started to be verbally abusive to my mother. This definitely did not help our family life, and we went from a form of "normalcy" before he was deployed to chaos once again.

I just couldn't understand why love wasn't enough for them. They talked about separation, and I saw the telltale signs that they were planning on getting divorced again. This caused me to become more and more distant from my parents. I started living in the future—dreaming about what life could be like instead of living in the present. I was in high school at this time, about fifteen years old, and felt like things would never get better. We went through the entire divorce process again, and this time I was old enough to participate in the divorce procedure by taking the stand in court. The pressure of being in the middle between my parents was overwhelming.

Who do I please?

Whose side do I take?

Thankfully, I was surrounded by people of faith. The divorce procedures went on for over a year, and in the end, my mother gained full custody of my siblings and me. Even so, my mother was still very distracted by my father's harassment. I was often left to my own devices and friends, and I didn't have much supervision. I strongly believe that the Lord provided me with a hedge of protection in my friends of faith and my church. By this time, I was also motivated, completely focused on a way out. I invested myself in activity. A busy and packed day planner would be my out. School, sports, work, church, all to keep busy. Little did I know at the time that busyness would become my default coping mechanism whenever I was under pressure. It served as a diversion of my attention. This would later play out in my life as an unhealthy mechanism to deal with my emotions.

The next couple of years were somewhat of a blur for me. But believe it or not, by the time I was seventeen years old, my parents were back together, mostly for convenience. By then, my father was retired from the military and doing some odd jobs. All I could think about was graduating from high school. At this point, I just wanted to get the hell out of Dodge, so I signed up for the military.

The emotional ramifications of going through my parents' three divorces, hoping for some kind of happy ending, took a toll on me. I never felt like I could please either one of my parents, and that translated into other areas of my life. As a kid, I was already trying to deal with the normal challenges of growing up, so adding the pressure of my parents' roller coaster relationship and continual drama caused me to shut down emotionally. When you're not being cultivated at home, it leaves you vulnerable to be cultivated outside of the home.

Recalculating

Sirius XM Channel 63, "The Message," has an advertisement that says, "You're never too far gone. _Recalculating_. You have arrived at your destination." God provides a way. He promises that. Whether we make choices or others make choices that steer our life in certain directions, we are _never_ too far off the path. We can always recalculate and recalibrate our position to the right path.

> We can always recalculate and recalibrate our position to the right path.

My childhood and my parents' divorces presented multiple paths for my life to travel. I'd be kidding myself and you if I said that I didn't dabble in bad behavior. However, the Spirit in me always knew and convicted my heart. I knew when I was doing things I shouldn't. It breaks my heart that so many people today _don't_ know. They don't have the knowledge or guidance of the Holy Spirit to help them recalculate their path.

I am so thankful that, even though I was entrenched in my parents' dysfunctional relationship throughout my childhood, God placed people in my life who would have a lasting impact on me, such as our neighbors across the street. Every Sunday, they would load up their big conversion van to go to church and would always take me with them. It might not have seemed like a big thing to them, but it was major in my life. Sometimes we don't realize how far those little acts of kindness will go in someone's life. Them inviting me to church offered me that little bit of hope and the Lord's guardrails that helped me get through all the challenges at home.

Going to church exposed me to hope that I didn't even fully understand, but I can't imagine what decisions I might have made or what things I might have done if I hadn't been clinging to the idea that there was something (Someone) greater than what was happening in my life. Each week, I heard about the hope that comes when we put our faith in Jesus. The message they preached was more enticing than some other influences that could have pulled me completely down those more destructive paths. I'm so grateful to those families. They were obedient in their walk with the Lord, and I will never forget their kindness and the interest they took in looking out for me. God provided exactly the care that I so desperately needed.

"When my father and mother forsake me, then the Lord will take care of me." (Psalm 27:10, NKJV)

I know now, being a parent myself, that my parents did not intentionally ignore my emotional needs. They were just so caught up in their own needs that they never really recognized how everything was affecting their children. So, for me, church became my safe place, a refuge I so desperately needed. I remember my neighbor giving me this tiny children's Bible—you know, the pocket-sized New Testament written in the King James Version. I would go to my room and climb under the tent I made with my covers and hold on to that Bible for dear life. I wanted to be in my own isolated bubble, away from everything. That tent, with my toys and my tiny Bible, became my safe place at home. Whether I could read it or not, that tiny Bible represented truth from God's Word. Though I didn't totally understand what I was reading in my Bible or hearing at church, God made sure that it got translated into my heart language. Both church and the Bible provided hope and gave me the fuel to persevere through the drama in my family that I had no control over. Even as a small child, this foundation of faith was powerful enough to give me confidence to get through some of the mistakes I made later in my life (which I will talk about in another chapter).

Being taught, and allowing ourselves to be "learnable," opens our hearts to a new world. It lets us find the scenic routes on our maps, enjoying each moment of the journey. I love to use analogies, so here goes one of many in this book. My husband taught me about biodiesel fuel and how old cooking oil is converted into usable fuel. This concept is fascinating to me, mainly because I love to look at situations and turn them into life lessons or something profound. It's not that you can put the dirty cooking oil directly into a diesel engine. There is a very specific refining process it must go through first, but it can be used again. The refining process turns what was old, dirty, and seemingly useless into fuel that can take something somewhere. It has been repurposed.

All that mess in our lives growing up is like old dirty cooking oil that was being refined and repurposed into fuel for us to keep going, to excel, instead of giving up and thinking that what we saw at home was all life had to offer! I'm thankful that God has a way of refining our *mess* and repurposing it into His *message*![1] Our past does not have to dictate our future. Instead, it can be the very thing that becomes a catalyst for change in our life. Don't underestimate the little things in life that bring a sense of hope and clarity in the fog of dysfunction.

When we allow the truth in God's Word to fuel the course of our life, we will be unstoppable. I love what the Apostle Peter says in 1 Peter 5:10:

> *"And the God of all grace, who called you to his eternal glory in Christ, after you have suffered a little while, will himself restore you and make you strong, firm and steadfast."*

PIT STOP PRAYER

Dear Heavenly Father, we praise You for who You are, God ALMIGHTY. Thank You for loving us so much and for relentlessly pursing our hearts. You made us to know You and find You.
Lord, we bring ourselves before Your mercy.
Please forgive us for ignoring Your repeated invitations because of our affections and distractions. We lift up families and marriages that need Your guidance.
Lord, provide a Christ-follower for those children who need to see Your invitation and to receive the hope that only You can offer. In Jesus' name, Amen.

YOU ARE HERE GUIDE

Your Rearview Mirror

1. Can you recall something from your childhood that has had a lasting impact on your life? If so, write out that memory and how it still affects you today.

_____

_____

_____

_____

_____

_____

2. Who was involved in that memory? Are you still in relationship with them now? Why or why not?

_____

_____

_____

_____

_____

_____

_____

_____

_____

_____

_____

_____

3. Can you remember a time when the truth in God's Word gave
   you a feeling of hope and confidence that allowed you to see
   beyond that situation? Explain.

_____

_____

_____

_____

_____

_____

_____

_____

_____

_____

_____

_____

_____

4. Growing up, did you have a safe place? Explain.

5. As you read through Chapter 1, is there something in your life that you feel God wants to refine and repurpose? Write it below.

MILE MARKER 2

No Outlet

*When you let pride
lead you rather than truth.*

We get into messes sometimes. Yes, sometimes things happen to us, but sometimes, circumstances happen because we make poor decisions from a place of pride. Unfortunately, when we make those decisions, we end up in situations that require us to get out of them. In the words of Dr. Seuss,

> I'm sorry to say so
> but, sadly, it's true
> that Bang-ups
> and Hang-ups
> *can* happen to you.

> You can get all hung up
> in a prickle-ly perch.
> And your gang will fly on.

You'll be left in a Lurch.
You'll come down from the Lurch
with an unpleasant bump.
And the chances are, then,
that you'll be in a Slump.

And when you're in a Slump,
you're not in for much fun,
Un-slumping yourself
is not easily done. [1]

I love that Dr. Suess says "un-slumping yourself." You see, we have
to undo or "un-slump" ourselves. The question to ask is— how did
we get into the situation in the first place? And when we un-slump,
what can we do to keep from slumping again?

Pride is deceptive, like a *"No Outlet."* It's really a
"Dead End" in disguise. While a *"Dead End"* is
straight and to the point from the onset, a
"No Outlet" lures you in, hinting at turns and
alleys, a maze to be discovered. It
invites you to figure it out. Sometimes
you can even see a nearby neighborhood or
the park you're trying to get to, and from
where you are, it appears that the sign is
wrong. You tell yourself, "I can get there.
It looks like there is a cut-through!" With
this deceptive invitation of what appears to be a
way through, you traverse the maze, only to find yourself
having to return back to where you started. Pride and deception
are our *"No Outlet."* We lose ourselves in a maze of pride to
avoid facing the truth of our own decisions. We pretend we

know exactly where we're going in an attempt to deceive others and earn their acceptance. We want people to believe we are a certain way, just like a *"No Outlet"* tricks us into believing it will lead us where we want to go. But in the end, trying to go our own way only delays our journey.

This is where we "do our own thing." We think we know best—or maybe we just want a little diversion from the main path—and so we choose to ignore the signs. We kind of feel invincible. But we also discover that as we travel these roads, we can easily lose our positioning and our way back.

Usually, we are looking for some spark of excitement. Maybe the main road is boring, straight, and dreary, so we decide to veer off and go see the sites on the scenic route.

We desire passion, excitement, but if we follow the wrong kind of excitement or if our gauge of what is exciting is off, then what we think will lead us to an exciting adventure may turn out to be a road to nowhere.

We spin our wheels and feel like we have made some progress, only to find out we're right back where we began. Even when we physically separate ourselves from the drama and dysfunction, it seems to travel with us in our hearts and minds! Our past can keep us in neutral, both emotionally and spiritually, if we allow it.

Looking In My Rearview Mirror

Most of the memories of my family life centered around fighting, alcohol, physical abuse, and harsh punishments—all behind closed doors, of course! I'm not sure if adults think that kids aren't listening or don't really understand what's going on, but I heard and understood. It was the feeling of hopelessness that led me to learn how to pray! God got a hold of me early on, as if He was preparing me for what was to come. In my little isolated bubble, I began to talk to God, "If You're real, then please make this all go away like it never happened."

That prayer was never answered, but it was the innocent prayer of a child. I began to learn very quickly that my life would not be like the "other kids." My life was destined to be different. I soon discovered that "different" meant "isolated." My trust in my parents dropped drastically. Between my father's drinking and my mother's anger, it was very hard to attach myself to someone who was barely hanging on in their own life. That inability to attach myself to someone or something would linger for years.

When something is not the way we expect, we spend a lot of time dreaming about the what-ifs, what was supposed to be, asking questions about why it's not the way we wanted, rather than accepting what is. We all handle the rough times differently. I vaguely remember that my older brother handled the difficulty at home in a similar way. Like me, he hung out with friends and got involved in sports and outside activities to keep his mind occupied with other things. But my younger brother acted out a lot. He became destructive, hyperactive, and a loose cannon. Unfortunately, without help these patterns of behavior in our younger years can set the tone for the rest of our lives.

As I shared in the previous chapter, I was graciously exposed to Jesus very early on, through our neighbors. I was strongly attracted to the interaction the family members had with each other. The heart of their family drew me close to them—a spirit, an aura, if you will. Little did I know at the time it was the Holy Spirit in them, but I knew that whatever they had, I wanted. I went to church, and I quickly received Jesus as my Lord and Savior. The message, "Jesus can heal your pain. He can take it all away," was exactly what I was looking for in my life.

But nothing seemed to change. I felt jaded and confused.

Where are you Jesus?
Why does my heart still hurt?
Why are my parents still fighting?
Why am I still being yelled at?

I entered that relationship with Jesus conditionally. I would trust Him if he delivered on His promise to take away the hurt. With pain still in my heart, I didn't turn my back on God, but I didn't do anything with my belief in Him. I decided to take control over my own life. I tried to find ways to do my own thing as if I knew what was best, because when control was in my parent's hands, it left me not trusting anyone…even God.

Caution Fog Ahead

I felt very lonely, because I had no "real" friends. Not that it was their fault. I wasn't a real friend myself. I didn't know what it meant to be loved unconditionally, so I loved conditionally. It was like my soul had no heartbeat. It was going on, living and breathing, but I had no joy. I was merely existing and surviving.

Even at a young age, I tried controlling everything I could, looking for worth and value in many things. At fifteen years old, I started experimenting with drugs, alcohol, boys, and *work*. Oh my goodness, I worked so hard and dove into being *excellent*. I wanted to be the best and recognized as such by others. I went to school and drowned my mind in knowledge, education, and accolades. All brought a temporary sense of satisfaction, but eventually the feelings of emptiness returned.

The pursuit of "other things" took control over me rather than the other way around. I was going to clubs and passing for twenty-one just to get a sense of relief from the pain I dealt with every day at home. I felt this pressure to do whatever it took to alleviate that empty feeling inside. But no matter what I tried, I always found myself back where I started. I let these temporary things deceive me and lure me into the "*No Outlet*" maze. I figured, I knew better than some silly "signs." I was all grown up. I was taking care of myself. My pride deceived me into thinking that I was smarter than the signs. But I wasn't. Every time I had to pass security with a fake ID, my stomach turned. My soul knew I should *not* be there. But the excitement, the jolt of adrenaline when I made it through, was intoxicating. Temporary, but intoxicating nonetheless. In those moments, that feeling was much better than the drama, hurt, and abuse at home.

For a time, those things did temporarily quench the hunger and thirst in my soul, but they never brought any real sense of satisfaction and joy. When the "high" wore off, I would see vague glimpses of my father's controlling nature and my mother's anger in myself. Not a very pretty picture. As much as I tried to change how I felt by trying this and that, wandering down the various offerings of a "*No Outlet*" maze, I always came back to that place of pain, rejection, and abandonment that haunted me emotionally.

Year after year, even into my twenties, I kept chasing fantasies of happiness. The patterns of behavior that I established in my youth continued into adulthood. It just became normal behavior for me, as if I had tunnel vision. But you can't just focus on your goals. You need peripheral vision to take in the surroundings and learn from your experiences and environment. If the definition of insanity is do the same thing over and over again, expecting a different result, I guess I was in a season of insanity.

Recalculating

Can you relate to some of my personal choices? The desire for a shortcut out leads us to take matters into our own hands. We don't realize that this is exactly what the enemy of our soul *wants* us to do. The choices we make can have some devastating consequences and even a lasting impact on our lives. Instead of the weight of pain getting lighter, we just start accumulating more pain from the things we attach ourselves to. This can be a vicious cycle that develops into a pattern of behavior, which then influences our character. Eventually, we feel like we have no way out—no outlet!

Thankfully, there *is* a way out. *Faith* gives us the opportunity to recalculate our direction. It's never too late to turn to the One who is the *way maker*. Our faith in Jesus is the only way out of the endless maze of bad decisions and attachments.

One of the benefits of looking back over some of our life choices is to learn from them so that we maneuver the remainder of our journey in a way that gets us to our desired destination. There's nothing we can do to change the past, but our past does not have to define us. We can use the lessons we have learned to refuel and get back on the road that God has purposed for us to travel on.

> It's never too late to turn to the One who is the way maker.

"Set up road signs; put up guideposts. Take note of the highway, the road that you take." (Jeremiah 31:21)

I have learned there are no good shortcuts or cut-throughs in life. Shortcuts only lead to misguided mishaps, deceptive delays, and twisted turn-arounds. It's much better to travel on the highway found in God's Word. All through scripture, God warns us about taking the right roads and staying on the straight and narrow path. His signs are clear, and they lead to life-changing hope. He alone can guide us out of trouble, and His GPS does not require constant updates. Unlike our car GPS that waits for us to make a wrong turn before recalculating, God doesn't wait. He knows us. He sees us, and He goes before us.

> *"See, I am sending an angel ahead of you to guard you along the way and to bring you to the place I have prepared."* (Exodus 23:20)

Nothing we have done can disqualify us from God's loving assistance.

No matter how long we have been wandering on our own, God is so faithful to provide a way for us. We don't have to be that person who doesn't ask for directions. All we have to do is humble ourselves and ask. Nothing we have done can disqualify us from God's loving assistance. We are the ones who put up the stipulations. Has your GPS ever said to you, "Sorry, you went out and drank too much last night, so we can't recalculate and put you back on your path"? No. Of course not. And God is so much more compassionate than a non-emotional machine!

Just as you wouldn't expect your GPS to deny your course correction request, neither will God. He has a way of providing angels in our life if we would only recognize them as such!

(I'll share in future chapters about a few angels God has sent my way.) It is unfortunate that we continue on the same road, trying to push ahead, not realizing that God has been sending warnings through people and unforeseen circumstances to get us to pull over and evaluate our course. The demands of life can muddy our windshields, all too often leaving us blind to the reality of our present condition. Instead of God's voice trying to set us back on course, the voice of poplar opinion becomes the only thing we hear as we let modern culture dictate our priorities.

If we are not careful, we will become just one of the statistics out there in whatever category we seem to fit into. But that's not the way it's supposed to be. That's not what God has planned for your life. Even if your faith is as small as a mustard seed, God can make that seed grow when you put your trust back where it belongs—in Him!

We have to learn to see our own pride and the misguided steps that we take through our own arrogance. When we make decisions not based on the truth that has been set before us, we put ourselves above God. Our own pride says we know better than God. We say to the signs, "Yeah, right." From what we can see, we think we can get to where we're going regardless of the sign saying, "*No Outlet.*" It's as if we know better than the ones who have gone before us, who have already gone down these paths, who have designed these roads. Somehow our pride says that we know better.

We're not supposed to fit into the culture of the world. Rather, we are to be a peculiar people, set apart! So, celebrate being peculiar rather than trying your best to fit in! (See 1 Peter 2:1-12, NIV).

PIT STOP PRAYER

Dear Heavenly Father, You are the Creator of our emotions. You know our every step and how we are going to act or respond before we do. We may fall into statistics, but You have made us unique, and our faith journeys are unique. Thank You for clearing the dirt off our windshields, the sin out of our lives, through the blood of Jesus Christ. We confess our sin of pride to You when we just can't get out of our own way, when we believe that we know better than Your direction and Your guidance and we have to learn the hard way. Our pride leads us down paths that we were warned not to go down, but we decided our ways were better than yours. Thank You for giving us the free will to learn on our own and accepting us back on the main road so that we can continue to follow You. For those of us who are either still wandering or need Your guidance to find our way back, please, Lord, help guide us back to You. In Jesus' name, Amen.

YOU ARE HERE GUIDE

Are You Chasing Something?

1. Can you remember a time you felt isolated? Describe how you felt. Was that isolation a result of hiding yourself from others?

_____

_____

_____

_____

_____

_____

2. Would you describe yourself as a dreamer or a realist? How has that description played out in your life?

_____

_____

_____

_____

_____

....

....

3. Was there ever a time in your past that you felt let down? If so, how did that affect the choices you made in your life either as a young person or even as an adult?

....

....

....

....

....

....

....

4. Are you chasing something that is "destructive" and has produced a consequence you might still be living with today?

....

....

....

....

....

....

5. Have you ever ignored a sign or nudge that you felt from God?
   Describe that experience.

   _____

   _____

   _____

   _____

   _____

   _____

   _____

   _____

6. Write out a prayer to God asking for His help in an area where
   you still need victory. Ask Him to reveal areas of pride in your
   heart that may be isolating you from fully experiencing
   community.

   _____

   _____

   _____

   _____

   _____

   _____

   _____

   _____

Winding Road Ahead

*When decisions others
make impact you.*

I have come to the realization that I'm most comfortable when I'm in control. But there are times in life that we are not in the driver's seat. Rather, we're the passenger along for the ride of our life! To this day, I'm a terrible "passenger" because of past experiences in my life where someone had control and took me down some weird roads that led to confusion and heartache. Those experiences were like the twists and turns on a *"Winding Road,"* coming up unexpectedly and making me feel sick!

Call me what you will: Type A, perfectionist, obsessive-compulsive, control freak. I've called myself every name in the book. Ironically, obsession with control does the very opposite. It actually contributes to *loss* of control! We lose the ability to have any spontaneity. We don't relax. We miss out on the experiences we could have if we let someone else lead. We steal the opportunity to grow from others when we don't let them lead, and we stunt our own personal growth, too. So why do we need control? Often, we take control because at some point in our life, someone else had control over us, and it left us disappointed. It put a grudge in our hearts that continues to drive our decisions, and now that fear and bitterness actually drive while our true selves ride along in the passenger seat. We give fear the keys and let it take us for a horrific, dizzying ride. So even when we think we've taken control, we haven't. When hurtful, disappointing things happen to us, it's hard to give control to anyone—even God, despite His invitation to fall at His mercy.

Winding roads have a way of really testing our trust.

One question I had to ask myself was, *How has my own misguided, false sense of control really worked out for me?* I had to dig deeper to discover why I was not letting go and letting God. What happened to me that left me with no trust for other people? *Why* did I not trust? That's what it boiled down to— admitting my lack of trust to myself and to God, saying, "Lord, I do not trust. I have lost that ability. Help me to trust."

Trusting is uncomfortable, especially when our trust has been abused. Every now and again, my husband takes a back road in our area called Seven Sisters. It a winding road with seven switchbacks that literally force me to brace myself in the car. Every time we go down this road, I get carsick. I get queasy, my stomach starts to turn, my hands sweat, and my knees get weak. I am subject to every sway of momentum in the car. When I have to give control to someone else—even when I relinquish my understanding to God—honestly, my body reacts with the same symptoms. Winding roads have a way of really testing our trust. Do we trust what is around the bend? Do we trust that every turn is another opportunity for us to stop worrying and trust the driver? Can we trust God to drive us through and out of those winding twists and turns in life?

The voice that says, "You're not good enough" and, "Nobody loves you," and "You're never going to make it"—they're all lies. Lies from the pit of hell. If we don't expose the voices and thoughts for what they are, then we may never understand that we are already free.

Looking In My Rearview Mirror

This story is hard. It's one of the most difficult things for me to share about my past, but please know there is a beautiful, God-glorifying, redeeming ending. One night when I was ten, at a family event, I was sleeping on a sofa bed in a side room with a door that led outside when suddenly a family member came home and opened the door that led into my room. I knew immediately that something was wrong with him. Either he was drunk or high on something! He came over to the couch and tried to lay down with me. (Maybe he thought I was someone else.) His speech was blurred, so I had no idea what he was saying. I didn't know what to do—I just froze. If I let him know that I was awake, I thought something bad might happen to me, so I just acted like I was asleep. Before long he was lying next to me, rubbing himself against my back, skin to skin. I tried moving positions, hoping he would stop if he realized what he was doing, who he was doing it to, and that it was wrong. He didn't stop. I was deathly afraid that he would go further than just rubbing against me. If I tried to resist, would he get violent and hurt me even more? I had witnessed my father getting violent with my mother. So, I just stayed in a frozen state, thinking it would have to be daylight at some point and people would wake up. Then he would have to stop! My inner voice was screaming, "STOP," but I couldn't get a sound out of my mouth because fear had me frozen. After all, he was older, and I was only a child. How could I tell him to stop?

Eventually, he got up, and I ran to the room where my parents were sleeping. The door was locked, so I just lied down on the floor right outside their door and slept there the rest of the night. I never told anyone about what happened that night, but I wrote it down in my diary. Even at that young age, I was able to write out the frightening experience. Several months later, my father found my diary, and when he read about what happened that night, he became very angry. The thing that hurt me even more than the actual event was my father wanted me to keep this a secret between us. So along with my trust and my body violated, my own father introduced deception and manipulation to me at a young age. A year after he found my diary, something happened within our family, and he used "the secret" as ammunition to leverage power over the situation. There were always arguments in our family. My father always needed to have the upper hand of power and authority. He would use whatever he needed to manipulate things to go his way. When he finally told my mother what he had read in my diary, she refused to believe it ever happened. She accused my father and me of teaming up against her and her family. So there I was at eleven or twelve years old with this horrible experience that was still not being dealt with. My parents never took the time to even talk with me about what happened. This only made me think that my parents didn't care enough to hear me out, and I just became more and more disconnected.

Like the sudden and unexpected twists and turns of a *"Winding Road,"* that situation made me dizzy and nauseous. It not only affected me and my relationship with my parents, but it also affected my mom's relationship with her family. The added tension in the family prevented us from getting together for holidays and the like. Along with everything else that was affecting me emotionally, I now felt guilty for the distance within the family.

Caution – Foggy Windows

Looking back on that incident now, after years of repressing the memories, I realize that even though some of the details are lost, I can still remember the way it made me feel as if it happened only yesterday. Details may fade, but the emotion is ever-present. I read somewhere that repression is like throwing a rock into a body of water and leaving it there. Years later when you retrieve the rock, the details—the bumps, the ridges, the rough spots—will be worn away, but the rock itself remains. That's what happens to those repressed thoughts of things that have hurt us. When we try to retrieve the memories, the details have faded, and we can only recall bits and pieces of the incident. We can begin to question what is real and what is not. That might be why so many people who have been violated and stay quiet for so long are sometimes not taken seriously and are asked if they have any proof of the incident when they finally speak up.

But the lasting emotional effect of the incident is proof enough for the victim. The impact of that incident in my childhood ran over into my adult life. Though I did everything I could to push it way down into a hidden place in my heart and memory, it somehow kept rising to the surface. Whenever I was held in a certain position, the flashback of that night would grab hold of me. It even affected my intimate relationship in my first marriage. Whenever my husband and I were in bed and he would press up against my back to "spoon" with me, it would bring back the memory of that night. I had to explain to him that if I could not see his face and only felt him against me, it made me freeze up. I'm thankful that he understood and was sensitive to my feelings. By the grace of God, I've overcome that feeling of fear, but it has taken me some time to work through it all.

Not only were there physical ramifications, but there were also emotional ramifications as well. Because my mother didn't believe me and chose *not* to address my emotional needs, it affected my view of authority. The very people who were supposed to protect me didn't. So I grew up having to be strong for myself. Since I didn't trust the authorities in my life, I didn't live under authority. I became my own authority! That mindset was a continuation of that *"Winding Road,"* full of unexpected twists and turns. Even though I thought I was in the driver's seat, the ride still made me feel sick! I was clinging to a delusional sense of control. I was driving, but my life had no speedometer, no gauges on my dashboard to alert me to trouble.

Recalculating

I know now that I was searching for a place of comfort where I felt safe and secure, but I always came up empty!

For some time, I waited and waited for things to change before I finally came to the realization that nothing would change until I did. But *how* could I change and *what* needed to change? Then one day I received a card from a friend, one of those kinds with a clever quote on it. This one had the Serenity Prayer!

God grant me the Serenity
to accept the things I cannot change
the courage to change the things I can,
and the Wisdom to know the difference.[1]

Wow! That prayer really made me think. There are things in life that we have to accept cannot be changed. We cannot go back and undo what has happened. But there are things that we *can* change, such as the way we let those events affect us. Only God can give us the wisdom to know the difference. Only God's truth and His view allows us to see that in the worst of circumstances, there is hope. There is His story to be told. It became a desire in my heart to have the courage necessary to change my perspective in many ways. I needed to change how I saw myself as the victim. I needed to be vulnerable with myself. I needed to ask God, "Change me. But first, show me. Show me where I need to change."

As if I wasn't sick enough from the twists and turns at this point, it got worse. God did just what I asked! He began to show me parts of my heart that I didn't even know existed. Ugliness that I had. Darkness that I was incapable of comprehending. But I had to go there in order to get here. Even though I had received Jesus Christ as my Savior, I don't think I had really accepted Him as my Lord! I think the lack of trust I had for authority in my life included Christ. After all, my parents didn't protect me, and I felt God didn't protect me either. Even though I went to church, prayed (usually as my last resort), and occasionally read the Bible, there was a real disconnect between God and me, just like there was a disconnect with my parents. They were still there in my life, but the relationships didn't have any real impact on the way I lived. But that was one thing that could change—if I had the courage to face up to some of my own issues.

True inner change takes time.

I had too much respect for myself to live the rest of my life as a victim. I knew in the pit of my soul that life didn't have to be a continual "*Winding Road*" that kept me feeling confused and sick to my stomach. There had to be more, and I was determined to change the trajectory of my life. I knew that healing was possible, but first I had to be willing to allow Christ into my life as Lord. If we're honest with ourselves, especially those of us who are control freaks, it's not easy to give up control. We say it, but we really don't follow through. There's just too many "what if's" when we consider the plans we have for our life.

I remember coming across this verse in the Bible one day while doing my devotions:

> "*He said to her, 'Daughter, your faith has healed you. Go in peace and be freed from your suffering.'*" (Mark 5:34)

I knew that God was speaking to my heart to reach out to Him for healing. I had no idea how long it would take! The time in between—this is the waiting place! We live in a world of instant. We can instantly change our hair color. We can drop color contacts in to change our eye color. We change our fashion, cars, homes, jobs, etc. These are all quick changes that instantly affect our circumstances. But true inner change, that takes time. We have to wait, and we also have to be faced with opportunities to know if the change really has taken place. I talk about this later in "*Detours.*" It's just like with children. When we correct our children, they may even be able to recite back to us what they are supposed to do, but only in the moment when they are met with the challenge again can we actually see if our correction stuck.

PIT STOP PRAYER

Dear Heavenly Father, thank You for Your compassionate heart. Help us have a heart like Yours and forgive those who have harmed us. Give us compassion for them and where they may be in their own journey. It's so much easier to hold onto the hurts and justify why we feel the way we do. But Lord, that is not Your way. Help us show Your love and forgiveness through how we treat others. Thank You for forgiving us of our sins and for forgiving those who have trespassed against us.

We ask for Your help in trusting You and trusting others again when we have been hurt. We ask You to give us clarity and courage to know You and follow Your direction, even when it's hard. In Jesus' name, Amen.

54

Dazed And Confused, and a lil' carsick

1. Can you remember a time in your life, either as a child or an adult, when you were the victim of some sort of abuse? Without going into too much detail, can you describe what happened?

_____

_____

_____

_____

_____

_____

_____

2. Would you say the memory of that incident is clear, or do you remember only bits and pieces of what happened?

_____

_____

_____

3. What lasting effect did that incident have on your life?

4. Read the Serenity Prayer. What do you have to accept will not change?

5. What do you need the courage to change?

MILE MARKER

4

Wrong Way — Do Not Enter

Defiance and the consequences of ignoring the nudge of the Holy Spirit.

ave you ever ignored a warning sign regarding a relationship, a change of job or location, a business endeavor, or even a health issue? Did you think something seemed right, so you ventured on, only to find yourself going the *"Wrong Way"* and colliding with emotional, financial, or physical destruction? I can totally relate.

When we disregard the warning and forge ahead anyway, we can experience life-altering setbacks that cost us a lot of energy and waste a lot of time.

Have you ever watched—or maybe even driven—a car going the wrong way down a one-way street? I have, both literally and figuratively. Neither are fun. And nether time was I in the right state of mind or heart. To be honest, the time I drove down a one-way street, I was intoxicated, and I put myself and my passenger in danger. Not a moment I am proud of. But the same happens when we travel down our life roads,

57

intoxicated by sin. We can't make out the signs. We can't see them with the chaos of our circumstances fogging our windows as we travel rocky roads.

Have you ever witnessed someone else going down the wrong path? Isn't it frustrating to watch someone make a bad decision? I cringe when I see it on TV or in real life. I just want to jump out in front of their car and scream, "STOP! Don't do this, please. It's the wrong way! Let me save you the trouble. Please, listen!" Yet they do it anyway.

It has taken me years to get out from under the weight of warning signs I have ignored in decisions I have made, including my first marriage. During a time when I felt angry and spiteful, I once again reverted to taking control of the wheel with little regard for my passengers. It was all about me and what I wanted.

> Our circumstances can feel like that bad storm—foggy, hard to see. We can't find our way, and even the signs are hard to read.

Have you ever driven in a storm? It's the worst. In the midst of the rain, the wind, and the traffic, it's very hard to see. The chaos demands you give full attention to the road, driving, and the direction of the storm, making it difficult to focus on anything else, let alone make decisions. In some cases, just when you think you are driving away from the storm, you realize it has moved directly into your path.

Our circumstances can feel like that bad storm—foggy, hard to see. We can't find our way, and even the signs are hard to read. We want our anxieties resolved and our inner turmoil calmed. As we search for that resolve and calm, we find or get ourselves in situations that seem to have no way out. We desire peace, but we settle for perceived peace. Our minds drown in fog, and we can't see where to go, what to do, or how to get there.

In the chaos and fog of our circumstances, we just want rest. It's hard to rest in the midst of the mess. I believed my longing for rest was my drive giving up. I thought I didn't have any fight left in me. But the reality was, the Spirit in me forced me to rest. You know those times when you just want to crawl in a ball in the corner of your closet? It's your heart saying,

I need my own time. I need to grieve. I need time to get this out. I need to clear out, so I can let in. Our bodies do this naturally, expelling the toxic waste in order to let more nourishment in.

It's no different for our souls and our hearts. Grieving, and processing, allows us to go through, get it out, so that we can let the good in.

We're often told to stop looking at the past, because it is done and can't be changed. I agree with that to a certain degree, but what I hope you find is a healthy way to "re-view" your past through God's eyes. You see, if we look at it with our small minds and our self-centered hearts, our past will always be a sob story. It will be the "woe is me" story, and, well, after a while that gets old and sad. But if we can look at our stories, our experiences, the way God does, then we can see beauty even in the hard stories. I want you to see the beauty in your "hard." Recognizing the beauty and the purpose in it takes the enemy's stinger off and replaces it with beautiful wrapping paper and a bow. It's like taking an old derby car and giving it a facelift—brand new doors, wheels, seats, and everything, on the same frame. You're still you, but all the dents and dirt from your past have been repaired and washed away, made new. In God's body shop, He repairs, replenishes, and rewires you from the inside out. But if we don't let God do body work on those stories, then they remain piles of junk cars in our backyards.

I had to learn the hard way. There were signs I didn't see, but God has re-worked this story for His glory. And my backyard is junk car free.

Looking In My Rearview Mirror

Growing up, my father was in the military, so you would think that I wouldn't want anything to do with military life. On the contrary, when I was seventeen, it seemed like the most natural course for me. I love structure, routine, stability, and at that age I still had a small dream of being an astronaut. One of the disadvantages of being a woman in the military (or some might think it would be an advantage) is that woman are a definite minority. My squadron alone had only half a dozen women to approximately two hundred men. So, there is the constant pressure of proving yourself not only to the men around you but also to yourself.

Being around that many men, you can become indifferent and see them merely as a force to be reckoned with on a day-to-day basis. But there's always that *one* who sticks out in the crowd, and for me, it was Andy. He was somewhat standoffish and made me chase him. Even though I liked the challenge, at the time I was very insecure and needed to feel beautiful and worth something. I always compared myself to other women, so it was important for me to capture the conquest.

After a few months of my provocative flirting, we started to get involved, but because we never had a lot of one-on-one time, the relationship was somewhat shallow during that season. He went on a TDY (Temporary Duty Assignment) for a few months, and when he returned, he was not himself. I approached him to find out if there was anything wrong between us, and that's when he totally blew my mind when he told me he was getting married. I was in total shock. He said he was marrying his best friend to "help her out." It wasn't a romantic relationship. It was just a very close friendship, and she need his help. That made no sense to me at all. It came right out of left field, and I felt so angry and utterly rejected.

Caution – Rocky Road Ahead

Once again, Andy went back out on a TDY for a few months. When he returned again, he came looking for me. And to my surprise, he was not married after all. Young, naïve, and vulnerable, I made myself easily available to him! Why? Because I was still so hurt. I have since learned that we need to be careful of decisions we make, and people we engage with, when we are in a state of hurt and vulnerability. Sometimes we need to stay in that waiting place, but as Dr. Seuss says, "Waiting, no that's not for me."[1] So, at the first sign of the tables being turned, I decided to give Andy another chance. This should have been my first warning sign (*"Do Not Enter"*) in this relationship, but I ignored it. Over the next year and a half, our relationship became serious, and we were married at the courthouse in San Antonio, Texas. Another sign in my heart that this was going in the wrong direction. Where was my wedding? No dress, no family, no reception, no cake. Just two witnesses. This was not how I wanted to get married. But I wanted Andy, so I settled.

A little side note: One of those two witnesses was the best friend. Andy's best friend! The very friend that he was going to marry instead of me. On the surface, I wanted to make amends. I wanted my marriage to appear like I had no issues with her and all was forgiven. Because why go into a relationship and marriage for the long haul and have animosity toward my husband's "best friend"? In reality, I was sticking it to her. I knew exactly what I was doing. I wanted her to sign as a witness on the marriage certificate. I wanted her to see *my* name as his wife, so that she would know exactly who he chose to marry, and not for convenience, but because he loved me. Are you seeing all the signs I am now, retrospectively? My goodness, these were some serious warning signs that I couldn't see! I was blinded by immaturity, naivety, and deceptive desires.

After our marriage, Andy was selected to serve at the White House and began to travel a lot with the Clinton Administration, so we moved to Maryland. My one concern was the promiscuity that so often took place when people deployed and traveled. He would tell me that he lost a lot of respect for some of the people he served with because he would see them have a relationship outside their marriage while traveling and then come home to be a "family man." The fact that he shared that with me helped me trust him. But you know what the Bible says,

> *"Do not be misled: Bad company corrupts good character (morals)."*
> *(1 Corinthians 15:33)*

It wasn't long before our marriage, too, was corrupted by bad company and bad circumstances. On a return trip, when I picked him up at the airport, I noticed he was acting very strange. He seemed distant, but I thought he was just tired. It was 3:00 a.m. after all. He acted like he didn't want to touch me. In the middle of the night I woke up to find him crying, and he kept saying, "I'm so sorry. I'm so sorry." I knew immediately that he had cheated on me. My worst nightmare. I had vowed never to let that happen to me.

When I'm hurting, I go straight into flight mode. I run away and physically remove myself from anything that reminds me of the pain. So that night, I did just that. I went over to a friend's house and shared what happened. I left Andy alone in the house to wallow in his own hurt while I cried with my friend. She just listened. It seemed that the world as I knew it had crumbled. Then numbness set in.

In time, I decided to forgive him. I attempted to give at least what I knew of forgiveness. I loved Andy, and I wanted peace. Fortunately, I knew a guy who could give us peace and bring genuine healing to our marriage. I trusted that God could heal our hearts. We started going to church and sought counseling. I did give him credit for telling me, and that was the open window for the healing that both of us needed. But even though I forgave him, Andy could never seem to forgive himself. That one thing changed our relationship and prevented us from getting to a place of true healing in our marriage.

Eventually, our relationship became lifeless and lost the chemistry and passion we once had. I felt emotionally vacant. In an effort to fill the void, we decided to take action. Instead of diving deep into the emotional potholes and dealing with the root of the issue, we told ourselves that we were missing the feeling of having a full on wedding ceremony. So, we did all that pomp and circumstance. Like most quick fixes, it helped in the short term, just like all external resolutions do. But I was hungry for something deeper, more meaningful—authentic affection and attention.

Andy's best friend was always there in the background. They were in constant communication, though she would never call him at home. It made me feel that even though he married me, I was always still the second choice.

His friendship with her became a point of contention. Eventually, I went looking to be someone else's first choice and started to go out when he was on travel.

At this time, I had gotten out of the military and had no real direction. It seemed I lost all source of stability in my life. Since I was getting excitement outside of my marriage, I started to consider that there was something better or different for me. I didn't want to stay in the stagnant stage of my marriage any longer, and I just wanted to get through it. Being young and inexperienced at the age of twenty-two, I allowed a lot of people to influence me, and I chose to file for divorce. Divorce is a hard word, and it's incredibly hard to go through. Andy and I had both come from divorced parents and didn't take it lightly. But I was convinced it was my best option in that situation. Aside from the process, the emotions, the starting over, the confusion, I think what hurt me the most was that he didn't fight. He didn't fight for me or our marriage. His response was, "If that's what you want." And like that, it was over. While our divorce was being processed, I moved back to Texas to get a fresh start. I went from living well with everything I needed and wanted, to having absolutely nothing. On top of that, during this time of transition and tremendous sense of loss, I also fell into a deep depression. Losing everything that I had invested in over the past five years caused me to go into a form of grief that I really didn't know how to handle.

They say there are seven stages of grief: shock and denial; pain and guilt; anger and bargaining; depression, reflection and loneliness; the upward turn; reconstruction and working through; and acceptance and hope.[2] I felt stuck in all of the first four stages, but the one stage that I found the hardest to move out of was *anger*. Anger at him, but also anger at myself. I was angry for investing my time and my heart into a relationship that made me vulnerable and needy. I always prided myself on being independent and intelligent. But after my divorce, I only felt stupid. And naïve for forgiving him in the first place when he was unfaithful to me. I felt duped once again. I dared to place my trust in someone, and that trust got trampled.

I grew even more angry! I was angry at people, all these humans hurting me, and I was angry with God. He let me down again. I placed all this trust in Him. I put my marriage in His hands, and He responded with silence. Back then (now I'm dating myself) "WTF?" wasn't a thing. But that's what I was wearing all over my face. I was angry, and I had no problem letting anyone who came across my path know it.

Recalculating with Guardrails

In Renee Fisher's book *Forgiving Others, Forgiving Me,* she stated, "Sometimes God uses sin to force us to start over."[3] Of course, getting a fresh start never turns out exactly like we expect. Getting a new job, moving, or making new friends might seem very exciting at first, but it takes a toll on one's emotional makeup. Let's face it. Who would want to be friends with an angry, negative, guarded, and self-centered person? Little did I know, this would not be the fresh start I was

Sometimes God uses sin to force us to start over

hoping for. But it was the beginning of something in me. I needed a new start. I just didn't know that fresh start would be forced by a combination of sin.

There I was sitting on the floor in the fetal position, crying harder than I ever had. I was alone and feeling very lonely. With my eyes closed in the darkness, I could picture what it felt like to be at the bottom of a hole. Every emotion within my heart was dark and dirty. I cried for hours. Lying on my back, I spread my arms up and cried out, "Take this from me, Lord!" I hated who I was and didn't know what I was doing or why I was doing it. Every day was like Groundhog Day, repeating over and over with no momentum, just regression. It all felt so meaningless.

I will never forget my time in Texas during the divorce. I just cried for what seemed like days. Naked on the floor of my apartment, as low as I could possible feel, I cried out to God, "Lord, it doesn't get any barer than this. I hate everything about the direction I am going in. Please help me. I'm in so much trouble. I am lost, blindly going through each day, masking pain after pain with sin after sin. Please, I need to know You are there. I need change. I need it badly. I can't live like this. I am free, but my heart is in prison."

Finally, the Lord brought the first signs of help to me. He made me realize I had to be open. I had to be willing to be vulnerable. And so I let one person in as a testing ground. Valerie Moreno was the person the Lord sent to me at this time my life.

This change was forcing me to get healthy, especially when it came to relationships. Soon after I arrived in Texas, God clearly knew what kind of fresh start I needed, and He was faithful to put someone in my path to help. He does that for us, putting people in our lives for a season, or, in some cases, for the long haul. To this day, Valerie is my one of my best friends. She became (and still is) a guardrail in my life, preventing me from going over the edge. She taught me how to have a healthy friendship. I had never had that type of relationship before. We were like two peas in a pod! Her friendship was my first glimpse of what "community" looked like.

With all the positive change going on in my life and heart, I started feeling like maybe I didn't want to get a divorce. Since I was changing, maybe our marriage could change. But Andy didn't want to get back together. He was stone cold. While a part of me still hoped for reconciliation since we were still communicating, I put my focus on growing stronger in my relationship with God. I began to learn from God's Word. I realized I didn't need to be perfect in order to be in relationship with Him. The Bible really began to come to life, and I began to see God's leading and faithfulness.

I stood on the Word and trusted God to change Andy's mind. But even though we never reconciled, I began to learn to follow God's lead, even when things don't work out the way I want them to. My trust meter was recalibrated through *not* getting what I asked for. My anger turned into peaceful understanding. The fog created by bitterness began to lift and make way for genuine healing. This was a real test of faith for me. God used the circumstances of this season to develop a faith in Him that I never had before.

Over time, I began to realize that the rejection I felt from Andy affected me in so many areas. I felt this pressure of offense trying to rise up in my heart, even in my relationship with God. The enemy of our soul always tries to accuse us to God and God to us. I was standing on God's Word, believing for a change in my marriage, and when Andy didn't seem to budge, it made me feel that God, too, was rejecting me. But I came across this powerful verse in Matthew 11:6, *"Blessed is the man who does not fall away (is not offended) on account of me."* This was when John the Baptist was in prison and, because of his circumstances, sent his disciples to ask Jesus, *"Are you the one who was to come, or should we expect someone else?"* (Matthew 11:3). Doubt had stirred in John's heart, but Jesus assured him that He was the One True God.

> **Doubt serves a purpose. It points us *toward* God, not away from Him.**

Similarly, doubt was stirring in my heart. I was doubting God and doubting my ability to have faith. But through continued prayer and studying God's Word, I learned that doubt serves a purpose. It points us *toward* God, not away from Him. I realized that I had to be willing to reflect back on the course of events in my relationship with Andy and admit that I had ignored one or more warning signs along the way.

"There is a way that seems to be right, but in the end it leads to death." (Proverbs 14:12)

It's so easy to blame someone else, even God, for the circumstances in our life, but we need to take ownership over our choices to ignore God's warning signs: *"Do Not Enter"* or *"Wrong Way."* One of the outcomes of turning a blind eye and a deaf ear to God's warnings is the pain of rejection.

Rejection, abandonment, and betrayal are like major potholes on the road of life. They can cause your faith to go flat, just like when you hit a pothole in your car. Whether it causes a slow leak or an abrupt flat, your journey gets sidetracked. Unfortunately, our faith life ride is full of potholes. Thankfully, we can learn to see these as temporary setbacks, not final outcomes. They make run-flat tires for cars now that allow you to travel several miles on a flat, but make no mistake, the tire still needs to be changed. Some of us are like those tires. We can go a distance after hitting a major pothole, but eventually, the change must happen in order to truly continue along our way. If it doesn't, it can possibly even cost us more to repair the permanent damage caused by ignoring the problem.

Humility is the key to learning how to follow God's leading versus our own opinions or feelings.

I believe that humility is the key to learning how to follow God's leading versus our own opinions or feelings. I read this in David Wilkerson's devotional entitled *God is Faithful*:

"A humble person is not one who thinks little of himself, hangs his head and says, 'I am nothing.' Rather, he is someone who depends wholly on the Lord for everything, in every circumstance. He knows the Lord has to direct him, empower him and quicken him – and that he is ineffective and useless without that direction."[4]

The key to humility is being teachable. All too often, our own pride causes us to live independent from God, making decisions based on our own reasoning, skill, and abilities. Simply put *pride* is independence, and *humility* is dependence. The Bible states, *"God resists the proud, but gives grace to the humble"* (James 4:6). The world encourages independence and believes it's a sign of strength, but in reality, it is one of man's greatest weaknesses.

As I learned these truths, I began to receive a peace about my situation. Purpose began to rise up in my heart. I realized the chaos was due to my selfish desires to change someone else so that I could be happy. Peace came not from someone else changing, but from my changed perspective.

I began to understand that I cannot control how other people feel. All I can do is control my thoughts, my words, and my actions.[5]

Reflecting back, I can totally recognize how my independent spirit caused me to ignore the warning signs in regard to my marriage to Andy, along with making so many mistakes over the years. Learning to yield to the road signs on our faith journey is essential to how we arrive at our final destination.

PIT STOP PRAYER

Dear Lord, You make no mistakes. You have laid out our lives, and You know what will happen well in advance. As we travel on our faith journey, there are some signs we completely miss. It is not Your desire that we experience the pain of divorce and heartbreak. But in our own decisions, we may experience this pain. We confess that we ignore the signs You give us and choose to fulfill our selfish desires instead. Thank You for putting people in our lives who become lifelong friends and even family. Thank You for being the one true relationship we ultimately need that heals all the broken areas of our hearts that yearns for relationship. Please help those in the world who are currently going through a divorce. Give them the strength to go through this season. For those marriages that need extra help, please heal them now. Thank You for the healing You are already doing and the stories that will glorify Your healing power. In Jesus' name, Amen.

YOU ARE HERE GUIDE

Learning To Grieve

1. Has there been a relationship in your life that caused you a lot of grief? If so, write out a brief description of the relationship.

_____

_____

_____

_____

_____

_____

_____

2. Were there any warning signs that you ignored along the way?

_____

_____

_____

_____

3. What potholes have you hit on your journey thus far?

4. Has God provided a friend, a helper, or guardrails in your life?

5. Rejection, abandonment, and betrayal are hard pills to swallow.
   What have you used to help you work through some of the pain?

R.E.S.T.

*Finding time to rest in
the midst of the mess.*

*M*ost of us are in a hurry to get to our destination. We have that nagging, child's voice in our heads constantly asking, "Are we there yet?" But even in the midst of our mess, God calls us to rest. It's in the moments when we stop to rest, refuel, and recharge that our minds and hearts can receive clarity for the future. Sometimes, we have to pull off the road, let the storm pass, and then continue a safer ride.

There's a reason why most major highways have designated *"Rest Areas"* where you can pause during your journey. Rest areas give you a safe place to use the restroom, get refreshments, stretch your legs, take a nap, make any necessary adjustments in the car, and plan out the next leg of your road trip. If you're anything like me, you'll browse through the gift shop and pick up a souvenir that will serve as a reminder of where you've been and the memories you've created.

So, let's take some time to pull into our emotional rest area and utilize all its facilities before we continue on our road trip together.

R = Relieve and receive

Hopefully by now you have recognized that you need to relieve yourself of a few things that you have been carrying around. Things like guilt, shame, and blame, just to name a few. These burdens keep us in the pain of the past, and we need to let them go so we can continue on our *life* journey. This is an area of personal responsibility. No one else can relieve us of the weight of our pain. Neither can *willpower*. Too many people try to relieve themselves of the pain of the past by their own willpower, and it never works. The only thing that will successfully enable us to move on is *grace power*. God's grace is sufficient, and it alone enables us to leave the baggage of our past where it belongs—in the past!

The Apostle Paul knew what it was like to have a "thorn in the flesh" that kept tormenting him. God gave him the remedy, and it is also available to each and every one of us.

> *"My grace is sufficient for you, for my power is made perfect in weakness." (2 Corinthians 12:9a)*

Paul's response needs to be our response:

> *"Therefore I will boast all the more gladly about my weaknesses, so that Christ's power may REST on me. That is why, for Christ's sake, I delight in weaknesses, in insults, in hardships, in persecutions, in difficulties. For when I am weak, then I am strong." (2 Corinthians 12:9b-10)*

By the grace of God, leave behind those weights that you have been carrying far too long, and receive greater hope and joy!

E = Evaluate and examine

Another important benefit of pulling into a *"Rest Area"* is that it gives you time to evaluate what you have learned and experienced on your journey. Life should never be a mindless existence of going through one day after another. As I have gotten older—and hopefully wiser—I've come to realize that *life* is a gift from God and should be lived with *joy* that comes from understanding the ways of God. It's only when we surrender our way of thinking and submit to His way of thinking and behaving that we experience real joy. It's been said that insanity is doing the same thing over and over again and expecting a different result. Evaluating whether or not you have learned the importance of surrender and submission to God's will and His ways is the first step to breaking that cycle of insanity.

After evaluating what you have learned and experienced, it might be necessary to really scrutinize your faith. Yes, you believe *in* God. But, do you *believe* God? There is a vast difference between believing in God and believing God. An honest answer to this question takes careful examination of our hearts and usually reveals itself during times of testing and waiting. To be a person of faith requires believing God regardless of what we see or feel.

"Examine yourselves to see whether you are in the faith; test yourselves. Do you not realize that Christ Jesus is in you—unless, of course, you fail the test?" (2 Corinthians 13:5)

I encourage you to take the time to evaluate and examine how you have been living your life thus far, and be willing to take the necessary steps to be a person of faith.

S = Souvenir

It wouldn't be a *"Rest Area"* without a gift shop where you can pick up a souvenir as a reminder of your visit and journey thus far. It's great to have a small memento as a keepsake. Hopefully this book will be that souvenir that will help you remember where you were when we started on this journey together and how far you have traveled. That's why I encourage you to take some time right now to write some thoughts that will be a source of encouragement for you.

MILE MARKER 5

Dead End

*Face to face with
the only final truth.*

ead ends. Decisions that lead to death. I learned many lessons during this phase of my life, but two stick out. Lesson one: Watch out for dead ends and turns that lead to dead ends. I got here not by one turn of my life wheel, but through a series of wrong turns. Thankfully, there is a way out of a *"Dead End,"* so stick with me. The point is, sometimes we need a *"Dead End."* We need to have absolutely nowhere else to go but to God. He is the One and Only Way!

Lesson two: Self-check. Ask myself, *Am I a "Dead End" for someone else? Is there something in my life that is not fruitful? Are there people in my life who I am not speaking life into, but death?* At first, it seemed the answer was no. Of course not! I could never. But after very close examination of my own heart map, there were things that made me realize I wasn't "all that and a bag of chips" like I thought I was. Reality check. My heart harbored things like negative self-talk. Gossip. Spreading sadness instead of goodness.

This is the woe is me story time, with no happy ending. Just poor pitiful me, not doing anything about my problems. What a joy I must have been to be around. Do you know anyone like that? Is that *you*?

You see, this is all the sadness the enemy wants to use to isolate us even more. To be honest, I was doing things that I didn't realize I was capable of. You know the "nevers" we say to ourselves, until we are in the situation, and then we say, "Well, this is different." Nope. It's not. It's the same thing that happened to so and so. Now it's happening to you, and it feels different because you now have a new take on judging people. This time in my life opened my eyes. Looking back with a different perspective (God's perspective) on this trial and this time in my life removed my judgment and taught me compassion. It taught me to reach in rather than judge from the outside.

Where I used to say, "Never would I ever," now I *did*. Perspective changed everything. It didn't excuse my behavior, and it doesn't excuse others, either. But it changes how we love others, how we relate and reach into their hearts and help them recalculate. They *need* help. I know that now, and since I have been through it, I can offer help from someone who "understands." Some people just need that connection. They need to know you actually know how they feel and can relate. Some just take help where they can get it. Neither is right or wrong. The Lord has made us all reachable in different ways. I can't reach everyone, but I can reach those who can relate to my story.

When you are afraid of yourself and the truth, it leaves you very weak, and subject to the most enticing of sins.

The words of this sign just reek of darkness with its "death" and "ends." We have no more choices in a dead end. We are left without options.

In this *"Dead End"* season, I was moved emotionally by things around me, but I wouldn't share them with others. This should have been the first sign that I was headed in the wrong direction. I had always been creative, a writer and deep thinker, but for this season, I kept it all bottled up. I thought I could handle it all with masks and smiles. I thought I was strong enough to keep up the façade. The reality was, I was afraid of my own thoughts. I was afraid of the truth.

When you are afraid of yourself and the truth, it leaves you very weak, and subject to the most enticing of sins. The enemy knows this. During this season of my life, I was at a complete dead end in every way, with only one lifeline. Without that, I promise you, I would not be here today.

One of my biggest challenges is being alone. Maybe you can identify. But being "alone" and being "lonely" are really two separate things. You can be alone and still feel the enjoyment of other people in your life. Being lonely even when people are in your life is far more difficult to navigate through. After all, doesn't the Bible say, *"Two are better than one, because they have a good return for their labor"* (Ecclesiastes 4:9) and, *"It is not good for the man to be alone, I will make a helper suitable for him"* (Genesis 2:18)? But I have had to learn that being in relationships completely depends on the people we're involved with and whether the relationships honor God. The enemy has a way of slithering in and disguising himself as a helper by way of companionship in our loneliness.

Looking In My Rearview Mirror

It was a moment that I dreaded as a working woman. I found myself involved with someone at work. Not only a work peer, but.... the boss! Someone with authority was going to disappointment me yet again, and here I was cornered. I had finally made a big break in my career and made the move I had worked so hard for. Little did I know, it was going to be one of the most life-changing moves I ever made. It all began shortly after I started my new position. I initially thought nothing of the gestures, but I knew the moment my boss put his hand on my shoulder (in a particular way) that something was about to happen. It was a gesture that, in my gut, I knew was inappropriate. Call it instinct, but more than likely the Holy Spirit was sending me warning signs!

Soon after that first physical encounter, we began having conversations that were far too personal. Because we worked together, we would travel to various work locations that would end with dinner and a few glasses of wine. Our time together was like a beautiful song that touched a very broken part of my soul. He pursued me, he entertained me, he gave me purpose, both physically and emotionally. At this time of my life, I was vulnerable beyond words. I was malleable, and I was naïve. I wanted so desperately to believe his words, his stories of hurt from his wife, and his perseverance for my heart. But there was a sliver of morality that I chose to ignore. With every glance from someone in the restaurant, I wondered if they knew what was happening. Did this look like a business dinner? It was meant to be a business dinner, but with the conversation and the touching, one thing led to another. In that moment, with all my past rejection and hurts, any attention I received was better than no attention at all!

I think he knew and understood my vulnerability because of his own hurt and rejection. So these two broken people entangled themselves emotionally, professionally, and physically. That relationship changed me forever. It definitely changed the trajectory of my life. My ex-husband wanted nothing to do with me, and this man wanted *everything* to do with me! I found myself in that place called *never*. I was numb and attention was my drug of choice. In that moment of *never*, I became addicted to superficial love.

I entangled myself in an affair with a man who was not only married but also my boss. Talk about a double whammy. I was more than disgusted with myself. I was afraid of myself at this point. Who was I? Who had I become? What a hypocrite I had become! All the while this was happening, I was in small groups, active in church, and singing in the choir. If anyone could "cover it up," I did it very well. No one had a clue. I say this because I know I am not alone. Someone reading this right now is covering it up, too. It doesn't have to be an affair. It could be any sin. We act like our worlds are perfect and fine, great and full of joy. But in reality, I was a hot, funky mess. Would I admit that? Of course not! You see, this pattern of behavior was taught. This was how my mother did things. Our life behind our home doors was hell. But the moment we went out, we put on a good face. *Act like we are a happy family. Laugh and smile, and put on all that fake!*

So, I put on the fake smile. My life became exhausting. And day after day, what life the church breathed into me on Sunday was sucked out by the enemy. But the Lord had a plan. He saw the enemy's prowling and started to pave a new road for me. It started with facing myself head on. I had to face what I had done. No more running away. This was the moment that finally built confidence in me, and to this day, I still rely on the memory of it. You see, looking back is not always bad. I look back on this moment now and realize, if I could do that— if I could really face it—then I can truly do all things through Christ (Philippians 4:13). Because it was only by His strength and grace that I had the courage to meet this death of myself head on and finally make a real, lasting change.

Caution - No Way Out

I remember the day very clearly. It was so hot! I drove four or five hours to the Outer Banks to meet a group of church friends for our second annual trip. None of them had any inclination of the hell I was living outside of that circle. That day, the trip to the Outer Banks seemed to take forever, but when we finally arrived at the beautiful beach house, it all seemed worth it. On the surface, everything was all I could ever dream of. I didn't grow up with the privilege of going to beach houses, so this was a treat for me. Here I was in my twenties and successful enough to be able to afford the gas to get there, the food, the excursions, and even the time. Unfortunately, from the moment I woke that morning, the clock ticked. My heart pounded, and almost every moment, I wanted to vomit. I was expecting a phone call that would put an emotional damper on this beautiful experience (or so I thought).

When we arrived at the house, we all unpacked and headed straight for the beach. In the midst of all the small talk and all the things you do on vacation, my heart was racing faster than it ever beat in any marathon or triathlon or sprint I ever ran in. I literally could feel my heart in my throat as I frantically looked at my watch every five minutes, awaiting the dreaded phone call that I knew would be filled with the never-ending list of lies in an attempt to validate what we did and why we did it!

The moment arrived. It was *her*! On the other end of the line, I heard the voice of the hurt woman, a wife, a mom, and for a moment I envied her courage and tenacity, her willingness to face me, the woman she probably blamed for the destruction and demise of her marriage and her family. She didn't sound the way I thought she would, and I'm sure I didn't sound the way she thought I would. Both of our voices quivered and trembled with the amount of adrenaline that was rushing through us. For about thirty minutes—which seemed like thirty hours—we shared the truth. My truth and her truth.

I told her all the things that he told me about her and their life together, and all the things he made me feel that gave me power, value, and purpose! With all the lies he told me, she added to the story all the lies he had told her. That conversation is one that not many people have. I was humbled and amazed that God would give us the opportunity to have the truth told, to have closure, and to ask for forgiveness. This conversation between us had started weeks beforehand through her getting my number from his phone, and eventually she reached out through social media messaging. At first, I didn't engage, and then one of her messages really got to me. I realized that if I didn't talk to her, I'd never be free. It was one of the pictures she sent me with her children. One of them was only a few months old, and it didn't take long for me to figure… What a liar he had been. That was when I told her about my baby. As a mom, she instantly empathized with my pain and realized that in order to move forward, we both needed this conversation. That is when we "scheduled" a time to actually talk on the phone. We were very real with each other and with ourselves about what we believed about the relationship we both thought we were in with the man we both thought we loved. Even more, it gave me a moment to really put my faith in God and His healing powers and to really test my belief in forgiveness and in the scriptures.

If there was ever a life-defining moment, this was it. Here I was, the mistress, the *other* woman, crying and ashamed, embarrassed and disgusted. In that moment, I was able to actually feel scriptures come to life. As I sat there on the beach, with the ocean in front of me, soaking in the vastness as the waves came crashing in, I *felt* how deep and wide the Father's love is for us (Ephesians 3:18). The waves crashed and pulled with every minute of our conversation, each wave as if God was saying, "*THIS*. What is happening between the two of you right now, this is forgiveness." Not only between us, but I also felt God's forgiveness. I looked out, and He just whispered to my heart, "It is finished. Your sins are at the depths of the sea in front you. You cannot see the depths of the sea. Go and sin no more." The pain, the embarrassment, the shame. With every roll of the tide, my eyes saw God take every bit of it and cast it out into the sea of forgiveness!

She and I never communicated again after that day. In the time we had, we said what needed to be said, and God did what He needed to do. My tears ran into the sea, and with each one, God washed me clean.

Recalculating

One of my favorite poems growing up was (and still is) "The Road Not Taken" by Robert Frost. The reminder of that poem inspired me to take my own "less traveled road." At this point, I wanted to make a difference. I wanted my life to matter. That meant I was going to have to travel down a path that most don't—a road of vulnerability. I'd have to face myself. I'd have to travel with God and discover who He made me to be. You see, we can travel the road of healing and move on with our lives. But the Road Less Traveled goes further. That is where we heal, we learn, and then we reach back and help others. I realized that what I was going through was not just for me. But remember, I'm an introvert. I am not that girl who goes out and gets out front. I dream of it. I practice it in the privacy of my mirrors at home. But me? Seriously, God? If He was going to have me travel this road, then He would have to pave it for me. The Lord does that. He helps us persevere past our problems so that we can have a positive perspective.[1]

I had nobody to blame for my decisions. After all, I was an adult, and it felt like everything was coming to an end with no way out. Up until this point, I had semi-mastered changing the outside—my appearance, career, where I lived, my friends. Those things were all so easy for me to change. But changing the inside, how I felt about myself, was not so easy.

Some people even considered it brave of me to move from place to place, adventure to adventure, but inside, very little had changed until I made the decision to take the Road Less Traveled.

I earnestly prayed that God would change the ugliness, the anger, and the self-centered desires that controlled me for so long. I relinquished control of my life, and every morning I was reminded that God has the power to take my breath. Instead of asking myself why things were happening to me, I started to ask myself why God had not taken me. I had certainly ruined my life. At the age of twenty-five, I was divorced, entangled in an affair, and directionless with my career. What was I going to do? Who did I want to be? Who did God want me to be? Who did He *make* me to be?

This relationship that led to adultery also led to an unplanned pregnancy. I was forced to decide whether to have the baby or not. As if traveling the road to Neverland wasn't hard enough, the enemy added a little extra darkness. I thought that if "he" wanted us to keep it, then maybe there was truth to our relationship. But the day he expressed his desire for me to not proceed with the pregnancy, my heart stopped beating. Anything I had left, just stopped. The enemy knew I needed that numb feeling to proceed with the ultimate never. After I made the decision to end the pregnancy, I came to a life-changing revelation, of one more never. I could never travel this road again. But how could I get out from under the shame and disappointments that weighed so heavy upon me because of the choices I had made thus far? All I knew was that if I could get through this with God, then from this point forward, I could trust Him to bring me to a new understanding.

The idea of a new life had new meaning. Part of gaining wisdom is learning from the mistakes you make along this journey called *life*. Through my mistakes, I discovered a new confidence and a yearning for knowledge, understanding, and wisdom, not in a "*Why is this happening?*" way, but rather to be able to give a word of encouragement to someone having a hard day. I began to realize that I did have value, and the most beautiful thing was when God revealed to me what wisdom looks like. I always thought that wisdom was something elderly people had. You know, that when they get toward the end of their lives, they could look back and provide these insights of wisdom. Wisdom didn't seem obtainable to me at such a young age. Then when talking to a hurting friend who was struggling with a certain sin in her life, a physical warmth came over my body, as if the Lord was standing right there with a hand on both of our shoulders. It was as if He said, *"This is why you went through all the pain, all the hurt, all of what you've experienced. It was for this moment right here, so that you can be My reflection to My hurting daughter."* I got to stand there and speak from experience so that she would know she was not alone. It was that very night, as I was driving home, that my calling was conceived. Where something else died in my life, God breathed life into me. I would become pregnant with hope and healing. He breathed something I had never known—confidence in Him and in what He was teaching me, to share and help others.

"And hope does not put us to shame, because God's love has been poured out into our hearts through the Holy Spirit, who has been given to us." (Romans 5:5)

PIT STOP PRAYER

Thank You, Lord, that You never leave us. We never have to be alone. You are omnipresent and love us no matter where we are and what we are doing. We make decisions that lead us to some far ends of the pain spectrum. Thank You for meeting us and finding us in this place. You never leave us. When we are at our wit's end and our dead ends, You are there to guide us out of our trouble. Lord, we confess our selfish desires and our failure to follow Your warnings. We ask that You make Your guidance and blessings to us clear. Please use us to be a light to guide others from their darkness and back to You. In Jesus' name, Amen.

YOU ARE HERE GUIDE

Shameless

1. How do you feel about being alone? Put into your own words the difference between being alone and being lonely.

_____

_____

_____

_____

_____

_____

_____

_____

2. Has loneliness caused you to make some poor choices? Explain.

_____

_____

_____

_____

3. Have you ever made a choice that seemed like there was no way out? Explain.

4. Did your choice affect others, and if so, how?

5. Have you ever dealt with shame because of a choice you made? Have you learned to get out from under the effects of shame?

MILE
MARKER
6

U-Turn

*God always provides a
way out and a way back.*

here are some choices we make in life that we know
almost instantly are taking us in the exact opposite direction
of where we should be heading. Sometimes we continue
on that road, hoping it might lead us somewhere beneficial. The
longer we travel in the wrong direction, the more we might
come to realize we need to turn around. We start to look for
the right place to make a "*U-turn*."

The Lord had answered my prayers to show me areas where
I needed to make major changes. But how to make those changes?
I knew what, but now the real action had to take place. Dr. Todd
Phillips of McLean Bible Church, the pastor of the church I
attended in my twenties, used to say often, "Knowledge without
application is supplication." Simply put, knowing without doing is
worse than not knowing. It eats at you. This is where the test of
faith really begins. Have you ever realized you needed to turn
around when others were in the car with you, and you were too

embarrassed to admit it? We do that in life, too. Instead of saying we made a mistake, we just keep trying to take turns that make the trip more complicated than necessary. It ruins the trip for everyone in the car. Even if it's just us driving, we can struggle with admitting we were wrong. We are embarrassed. I feel sometimes that embarrassment is a form of pride. It comes from assuming we are perfect or able to be perfect and not make mistakes. It's the impression we try to convince ourselves of and others around us. At the root of the definition of "embarrassed" is the word shame. We are ashamed. And shame is not from God.

I felt nervous about what I knew I had to do. I was nervous of the unknown. Sometimes we have been in our own misery so long, we have become so accustomed to our coping mechanisms, that it becomes the norm. It is comfortable. Even though the misery is terrible for us and our growth, it's what we know. We know it's bad to seek comfort in food, alcohol, sex, whatever vice, but we also don't trust that anything different will help. So we default.

This happens when we take the same route to work or to the store. It's known, familiar. My husband likes to take new routes, and it makes me anxious when we travel an unknown road, path, timeline. He disrupts my "known," and it used to be very uncomfortable for me.

This is the same when the Lord prompts us to make major changes or directional shifts in our lives. Especially when we have to turn from the sin that is the closest to us, right smack in the middle of our hearts.

My sins were isolation and presentation. I kept my real self in hiding and presented what I thought would be accepted and loved by others. I hadn't known any better, but I knew in my core that it was not the way I was supposed to live. You know how when you put two northside magnets together, there is tension? That was how I felt in my own skin. Sin and the Spirit cannot ride together, and the Spirit in me just had enough of sin junking up my car, changing the station, and messing with my GPS, so to speak. I was so done being all that I was not. I wanted to be REAL! I wanted to know what real love was. I wanted to be really known.

I was humiliated with myself for what I had done. But how could I be real if I didn't know who I was? This was where I knew I was out of *my* options. I had to seek outside of myself. I needed community, accountability, and Lord knows I needed grace like a fire hose.

There is a song by Cold Play called "Fix You." Its lyrics remind me of this stage of my faith journey. It was at my *"Dead End,"* in the darkness, that God brought lights to guide me home! When I lost my child, something I could not replace, and I felt nothing could bring me back to life, it was through confession that my bones were finally reignited.

Without confession, I could have continued to make wrong turn after wrong turn. As long as no one knew, I couldn't be held accountable.

But with confession, I would be taking the first step in holding myself accountable and setting myself free from hiding.

Looking In My Rearview Mirror

My affair and abortion took a major toll on me, both emotionally and physically. I felt very broken inside after the loss of a child. Some things in life take a lot longer to overcome and move on from. For me, I move on by keeping busy, and I invested all my time and energy into doing just that. I pursued external achievements like work, getting my master's degree, becoming a landlord, getting involved in the choir at church. But regardless of how busy I stayed, it just couldn't change how I felt about myself. Have you ever just been done with someone? Well for me, I was done with myself. I didn't like what I had become. The choices I made showed me to be so weak when I had always prided myself on being strong and resilient, as if that was a good thing.

I know confessing the affair to my boss's wife was the beginning of me facing up to what I had become. That was the first step toward making a turn for the better, but it didn't really deal with the internal struggle I was experiencing. I had to make a total turn around—a U-turn. A change of direction at this point was so necessary, because I felt like I was getting caught in a circle with no exits. I needed a drastic and complete shift in direction to reposition myself so my heart could receive the change God was trying to show me, but up to this point I had just been ignoring the signs. I would love to say it was a quick turn, but it wasn't. It was like turning a Mack truck on a bike path covered in mud. Nonetheless, I *did* turn the wheel of my life. I made the directional shift that was necessary and said good-bye to a road that led me to a *"Dead End."*

Why do you think we feel like it's too late to change our minds or direction in life, or that we can't turn back? I think we believe that people will think less of us if we change our minds. Then we are plagued with doubt about whether we really are on the wrong road. So we convince ourselves that maybe, just maybe, if we travel just a little bit further on the same road it will lead us where we wanted to go in the first place. Changing direction can be initially painful but vital for real change to take place. There's a song by David Dunn entitled "I Wanna Go Back." To paraphrase, the lyrics of the song proclaim: "I let things get far too complicated, my path of decisions led me to this place right here…and you know what… I don't like it so much. So I'm going back to a spiritual place and possibly even a physical place where I can find and know the truth."

Why do you think we feel like it's too late to change our minds or direction in life, or that we can't turn back?

Caution - Road Narrows

Finding the right place, the safe place, to change direction is important. One of the things that I invested myself in was the church choir, Total Praise. This proved to be a major turning point in my life and a blessing beyond words. I loved the sense of community I experienced as part of the choir. It was the heart of Jesus with skin on. God has always captivated me with music, but it was the community in the choir that really drew me in. Before I joined, I went to a few events with a friend who was in the choir. As a people-watcher, I would observe the way they interacted with each other. I had never seen anything like it.

It seemed surreal. At one point, I remember being angry because it looked so fake. But the Lord showed me that I was witnessing *Him* in action. It became overwhelmingly clear. As I began to build relationships, it became my "safe place." I knew I needed to talk to someone, so I went to my choir friend, Nate, and opened up about what I had recently gone through. Nate had a lot of wisdom, and I knew he would be able to communicate the truth in God's Word without making me feel judged. I needed to be brutally honest about myself, and he represented a very safe place for me. At a time in my life where I needed to trust, this was the most nerve-wracking experience. Remember, I had tried to talk to my family, my own blood, and was completely rejected. Taking this leap of faith to share my story with someone literally made my body shake with adrenaline.

One of the first things Nate told me was that I needed to confess this to the group that represented my community. He explained that I needed to *experience confession*. You see, confession has two parts: getting it off our chest, and then what God does with our confession. He suggested that I write a short list of people in my life that I felt I could trust. As I thought about who to talk to, I knew that I needed to include more than just the safe people who would make the confession easy. I knew I needed to challenge myself and tell those who I knew would hold me accountable. So, I put together a list of a few people in my community group and the choir and prayed over that list and those people. He drafted an invitation to the people on the list for a get together where I could open up and confess what I had gone through. The group was coed—one married couple, a couple dating, and the rest single. Why does that matter? Because sometimes we forget that people at different stages of life can all benefit from what we may be going through, as well as share their own wisdom with us.

One of the things I loved about being in the choir was that we did life together, so it wasn't unusual for Nate to orchestrate the entire event. All I needed to do was pray over what I would share. When the day finally arrived, I was shaking with nerves. I think I also vomited a few times. Could I really be so transparent as to disclose how I was in a relationship with a married man—my boss—and the difficulty of getting out of the relationship? In addition to that, sharing about the loss of my child through abortion made me too nervous to even look up. As I shared, I hung my head in total fear of their response. I finally lifted my head, tears clouding everything I could see, expecting disgust, shock, and awe. But it was me who was shocked and in awe! I was greeted with open arms, open hearts, and tears rolling down their faces. To this day, the memory of the grace I felt in that moment is what fuels my passion for you! For the first time in my life, I felt accepted! Just. As. I. Was! Ugly crying, shaking, snot rolling down my face. I felt one comforting hand after another, one on my shoulder, another grabbing my hand, another wiping my tears. This was the moment I had ached to experience my whole life. No one was disappointed in me. Instead, they all laid hands on me and prayed for me as well as praying for their own growth to help people who are hurting. One person in the group felt she had failed in being approachable and wanted to grow to be an accountability person for people in need. My mess, my confession, was used to heal not only me but others as well. God can use your mess to grow other people. When I stepped out in faith, God used my confession to help others grow, too. In that moment,

God can use your mess to grow other people.

the lights on my path grew brighter, and the direction of my life became clear. This heart was turned toward Jesus, and it was never going back.

I had never before experienced such a supernatural feeling of relief. After their support and prayer, I felt free from all the lies that I believed about myself. In that moment, everything changed. I never felt that kind of embrace and love before. I felt God pick me up off the floor and wipe the tears from my face. Through that group of people, He told me, "I'm here and have always been here." This was a life-changing moment for me as well as for the people in the group.

Recalculating

One of the best features of a GPS is that it doesn't shame you for going the wrong way.[1] It doesn't spend time re-hashing all the wrong turns you made. It doesn't go back and say, "Well, if you would have (fill in the blank), we wouldn't be in this mess." No. The GPS is more kind than that, and so is our Lord and Savior. He is kind to gently recalculate our direction and show us the way—His *"One Way"* that allows us to intentional clean up the mess we got ourselves into. It might be painful, but it is so necessary to look back at the mess in order to get clear direction to move forward. So often we think, *Let the past stay in the past.* But if you are on the wrong path, headed in the wrong direction, and you don't like where you are, sometimes making a U-turn and going back a few exits can reposition you on the right road that you previously passed by.

GPS doesn't shame you for going the wrong way.

With God, you can always make a U-turn. In Matthew 7:13 the Bible states,

> *"Enter through the narrow gate. For wide is the gate and broad is the road that leads to destruction, and many enter through it. But small is the gate and narrow the road that leads to life, and only a few find it."*

Though the road is narrow, it's never too narrow for us to turn our mess around, because our mess is never as large as we make it out to be. You see, Jesus settled the sin matter on the cross, so once you're willing to turn (repent), your mess is manageable in the Master's hands.

Most people don't realize that their physical health is very often affected by their emotional and spiritual wellbeing. Your body does speak to you, so you need to listen to it. Let me ask you, is there something off with you, either physically, emotionally, or spiritually? Do you feel like the two north/south magnet ends, resisting and creating tension? Do you feel like God is trying to get you to turn and redirect your path, but you are resisting? It's important to remember that our initial turn-around doesn't have to be our entire lives, just baby steps that will lead us in the right direction. The Apostle Paul states in Galatians 5:25, *"Since we live by the Spirit, let us keep in step with the Spirit."* Our turn-around is step by step!

But be prepared for opposition from the enemy. He does not want you to take the necessary steps toward God's plan and purpose for your life. The enemy prowls and tries to offer us a wide road out to lead us away from narrow road.

I love the advice Peter gives us in 1 Peter 5:6-11:

> "*Humble yourselves, therefore, under God's mighty hand, that he may lift you up in due time. Cast all your anxiety on him because he cares for you. Be self-controlled and alert. Your enemy the devil prowls around like a roaring lion looking for someone to devour. Resist him, standing firm in the faith, because you know your brothers throughout the world are undergoing the same kind of sufferings. And the God of all grace, who called you to his eternal glory in Christ, after you have suffered a little while, will himself restore you and make you strong, firm and steadfast.*"

Suffer for good or suffer for evil, but in this life, we will suffer. Better to suffer for good. This is a good time to pray to God about everything you are going through so that His peace will guard your heart and mind in Christ Jesus (Philippians 4:6-8).

PIT STOP PRAYER

Thank you, Lord, for being the God of grand plans. You are the master planner. Thank You for giving us the option to change direction and change our minds, so that You can change our hearts. You made us moldable, like clay in Your hands. Please forgive us for trying to make our plans higher than Yours. We ask for Your voice to be the voice we hear and follow. Sometimes changing our direction or changing our minds is uncomfortable and goes against the grain. Please remind us that it is not about what people think of us, but what You think of us. Lord, we pray for those who need a safe place. Please allow our homes, our hearts, and our lives to be a safe place where the hurting can find refuge and healing. In Jesus' name, Amen.

YOU ARE HERE GUIDE

Change Ahead

1. Have you ever been going in the wrong direction? What did you do about it?

_____

_____

_____

_____

_____

_____

_____

_____

2. Why do you think that in life we feel like it's too late to change our minds or direction?

_____

_____

_____

_____

3. Do you think people will view you as inferior if you change your mind/direction? Why?

4. Do you have a safe place to make a U-turn? Describe that place.

5. Describe the difference you feel once you start moving in the
   right direction.

One Way

*The one and only truth
gives us divine direction.*

The heartache and pain of previous mistakes and mishaps along this road of life can prove beneficial if we are willing to learn from them and change. Learning requires an open mind and open heart. So often, our past can cause us to become close-minded and guarded. We can resist going down the right road because it will require exchanging our opinion for the truth that can set us free! Sometimes we feel it's too late to change the course of our lives. But it is never too late to come to a place of surrendering your way for God's "*One Way.*"

Learning requires an open mind and open heart.

Sure. What a small word with such huge emotional impact! Almost immediately after we experience a miraculous emotional healing moment, such as with my confession, the enemy tries even harder to make us doubt the truth of what we have experienced. Literally the moment we all went on our way, I began to think, *Oh my goodness, what are they all saying about me now? What if that was just a front? What if no one talks to me anymore? What if I am shunned?* Isn't that exactly what Satan did to Jesus, prowling as He prayed the night before His crucifixion? Satan tries to make us unsure about God's truth.

So how do we become sure? How do we know we are on a solid path, the right path? Simple. We check with our trusted Navigator. The Lord gives us more than just a GPS to get us back on His way. The GPS is the Holy Spirit, who is gentle with us when we need redirection. He also gave us a map. He gave us directions. Unfortunately, we tend to shove that map under the seat (on a book shelf or in our nightstand) and not use it. We try to be our own map and create it as we're traveling, but then we miss the big picture of our destination.

We have purpose. Our mess has purpose.

Being sure starts with being open-minded and open-hearted. We first just have to open the door to our hearts and, as mentioned in Chapter 1, invite God in. He will not force Himself in the door. Inviting Him in gives us the security and safety we need. He has made us that way, with an innate need for a safe and secure place. With that, we can be free to experience His truth in our lives and take time to reflect.

Reflection gives us time to think and deliberate with God. To invite Him to really paint the picture He sees of us and to show us truth that we can stand on, truth we can hold onto. Truth even about our messes, our past, and His truth about what He wants to do with those messes. We have purpose. Our mess has purpose. It's not to shame us or repeat the past, but it's to share His power through our stories.

We have to decide. We are given the free will to make up our minds and invite Him in. That decision can come from simply asking God through prayer. When we want to make decisions, we usually go and research information. We want to be sure—as sure as we can be, anyway. God provides "sure." He provides information we can use to make the decision to follow Him.

Looking In My Rearview Mirror

One night I was at home, working on some assignments for my degree. I found myself having a hard time concentrating on what I was doing. I kept trying to get focused, but there was a pull in me that was not going away.

In my frustration, I stepped away to spend some time in prayer. While I was just going through my normal "routine" of prayer, "Dear Lord, help me with my attention deficiency right now…,"

I felt the Holy Spirit move over my mind and heart. Everything in the room and within me became very still and quiet. I realized in that moment, the Lord had been the one pulling me away. I began to cry. With my eyes closed, my mind and heart literally showed me a vision. It was like those flashback moments in movies. In a series of flashes, God showed me that He knew I was questioning in my heart, needing assurance.

I had never known what it was like to have a "vision" until that moment. It was a vision of all the people throughout my life who had a spiritual impact on me. It was as if they were all signs along my road. They were all a part of my journey, and even though I followed some and drove right past others, the Lord showed me where He truly was with me and guiding me the whole time. It seemed that they all were put in my life at different times to help me find my way out of all the fog and confusion that controlled me from my childhood through early adulthood. The family across the street that invited me to church, the families that took me in, the friends who befriended me as a child, the family that took me in during high school, the friends who invited me over for dinner, the prayer warriors when I needed intercession, the choir, Valerie...the list seemed to be endless. It was as if God was pointing out, "This was Me, and this was Me, and this was Me. I, the Lord your God, orchestrated every single road sign in your life." I felt so unworthy. I was overwhelmed that He loved me so much to show me that.

> *"This is what the Lord says, 'Stand at the crossroads and look; ask for the ancient paths, ask where the good way is, and walk in it, and you will find rest for your souls.' But you said, 'We will not walk in it.'" (Jeremiah 6:16)*

This vision made real God's faithfulness to me through the people He sent my way. It was so clear, and I became grateful for His love and concern for me. The vision was like watching a movie of my life. Even though I took a lot of twists and turns that led down the wrong way, God always sent someone to say something or do something to get me to see the right path again. That vision made it so clear that there is really only *"One Way"* to go on this road called life. That way is God's way—directed and guided by His Word and the Holy Spirit. I knew that I needed to surrender my opinions for *truth* and that meant I would need to be more attentive to His voice.

> *"Whether you turn to the right or to the left, your ears will hear a voice behind you, saying, 'This is the way; walk in it.'" (Isaiah 30:21)*

This vision was something so supernatural that it filled my soul with overwhelming hope for my future. Knowing God's unconditional love and amazing grace filled me with great joy! It loosened the grip of my own need to control my life and gave me the freedom to trust God for whatever the road ahead held.

The Road That Leads to Joy

I felt ready to make the transition from being merely a believer to becoming a true follower of Jesus Christ. God's Word really started to come alive to me and inspired me to get my priorities in order. But I knew it would require me to lay aside things that had become a distraction, things like my past relationship with Andy. I knew it wouldn't be easy. I sometimes found myself wondering what he was doing and with whom. It became a major distraction, both mentally and emotionally. Talk about distracted driving! But I knew allowing God to do a new work in me required me to be intentional in not being sidetracked. It wasn't sinful to think about the possibility of us getting back together, but it had become a major weight that was hindering me from moving on with my life. Sin is not the only thing that can sidetrack your faith journey. The distractions that become personal priorities can also sidetrack us. These distractions may be good things, but they can monopolize your time and energy from truly following after God.

For me, this distraction hindered moving forward in my faith, because I felt like my relationship with God was dependent on whether God would put my marriage back together or not. I tested God, "If Your Word is so true, then do this! And do that." God was able to show me that was not the way He was going to demonstrate His power. As much as I wanted Andy's heart to change, it was in my heart and in seeing my desires change that His truth and power became so real. I was not made to tell Andy's story. I was made to tell mine.

> *"Therefore, since we are surrounded by such a great cloud of witnesses, let us throw off everything that hinders and the sin that so easily entangles. And let us run with perseverance the race marked out for us. (Hebrews 12:1)*

I began to realize that if I wanted to follow after God, I would have to relinquish control and hand over the steering wheel of my life to Him. Of course, that's not as easy as it sounds. It can be scary to let go because it requires a tremendous amount of trust. I had lost that trust somewhere along the way, but remembering how the Lord had been faithful in the past, even when I turned a deaf ear and a blind eye, helped me begin to trust again. This time, I wasn't trusting in my strength but rather in His strength. The chorus to the song "Jesus Take the Wheel" by Carrie Underwood says it all. He saves us from the road we are on, when we chose to follow Him and let go.

Recalculating - proceed to the road that leads to joy

I love the simplicity of the *"One Way"* sign. It's black and white. No gray area here. Making a decision is the same way. We either do or we don't. Choosing to travel down that *"One Way"* road is the first step. Every step after that will require the all-sufficient grace of God. Without God's amazing grace, it's impossible to travel down that road because sometimes we just cannot see where it will lead us. Once we let Jesus take the wheel, we will start to experience a peace that passes all human understanding and a joy that is undeniable!

Practically speaking, the joy comes from really getting to know God. The only way (pun intended) for me to do that was to learn. Learning was what I knew how to do best. If I didn't know something, or I wanted to figure something out, I found the information. In this case, as simple as it sounds, that meant reading my Bible. Notice I didn't say studying the Bible. I wasn't writing a research paper on God. I wanted to *know* God, which meant I needed to spend time with Him. That took shape in reading the Bible. I literally would just open it and read whatever and wherever it opened. Then I started to have fun with it. I'd close my eyes, run my finger all over the page, and then randomly stop. That was where I began reading. Even then, it could seem overwhelming. What a massive amount of information there was to get through, but I knew it wasn't something to read front to back. We don't get to know people by starting from the top of their head down to their toes. We start with the heart. Which meant I had to start with God's heart. I had to trust from the onset that He was still the God who had orchestrated divine events in my life, and He would orchestrate where to start getting to know Him.

When you are open-hearted and open to God's navigation, joy will jump off the pages of His Word and into your heart.

There is never a time I open the precious Word of God and am not just moved to tears by what jumps off the page and hits my heart. It's that feeling when the words speak to your soul, the essence of you inside, and you're like, *Whaaaaaat?* It's also very easy to get into the Word and find what you're looking for to validate yourself or your actions, but that's another conversation. When you are open-hearted and open to God's navigation, joy will jump off the pages of His Word and into your heart. It's that same joy and ease when your GPS gets you back on track and you breathe that sigh of relief.

I go to my ultimate road map for the same relief.

As I mentioned earlier, we want assurance. We want a positive confidence that God is real, that He is guiding us and will never leave us. I can't give that to you, but I can challenge you. I can and will pray for you. He has a special map for you. The more you fill your thoughts with the truth of scripture, the more confident you will be in where you are headed. Ironically, it may even come through others. God has the best sense of humor. Through my devotion to the Word, when my own mother came to me for advice or called to talk, she was always met with scripture and an inexplicable joy that came through my words. Though she had heard the Word from her friends and family, it was me God used to lead my mother to accept Christ as her Lord and Savior. I believe it was the change she saw in my life that caused her to open her heart not only to believe in God but believe Him for her own life.

Joy gives us the strength to go God's way.

Joy gives us the strength to go God's way, so it's so vitally important to come to an understanding of the "joy of the Lord." I started to understand that joy comes from our inward fellowship with the Lord, not from our outward circumstances. The more time I spent in prayer, the Word of God, fellowship with other believers, and sharing my faith with the people in my life, the greater measure of joy I experienced.

PIT STOP PRAYER

Dear Heavenly Father, thank You for making Yourself known to us through dreams, through random acts, through miracles, and through the divine ways in which You reach us. You don't have to make Yourself real to us, but You do through Your amazing love for us. Lord, we lift up the distractions in our life that keep us from experiencing just how real You are. Our busyness, our own earthly agendas, our egos, and our sinful desire to have more all distract us from serving You. Help us, dear God, to have our priorities align with Yours. Show us where they are not and help guide our hearts and spirits toward Your way. Grant us courage to let things or people in our lives go to make room for You in our lives and in our schedules. Show us a life where our desires are from You and not from us asking for Your blessing. Rather, bless us, Lord, as You so desire and remind us to always be a blessing to others. In Jesus' name, Amen.

YOU ARE HERE GUIDE

Lane Change

1. Can you remember a time in prayer when God made Himself real to you? Explain.

   _____

   _____

   _____

   _____

   _____

   _____

   _____

2. Is there someone or something that you have been holding onto that has become a major distraction to you and prevents you being willing to take the "*One Way*" road? Explain.

   _____

   _____

   _____

   _____

_____

_____

_____

_____

_____

_____

_____

_____

_____

3. Is your priority list in the proper order? What, if anything, needs
   to change?

_____

_____

_____

_____

_____

_____

_____

_____

_____

_____

4. List one particular scripture that has truly inspired you to make
    a change in your life.

    _____

    _____

    _____

    _____

    _____

    _____

    _____

5. Are you ready to allow Jesus to take the wheel of your life? What
    would that require from you?

    _____

    _____

    _____

    _____

    _____

    _____

    _____

    _____

    _____

MILE MARKER

8

Road Work Ahead

Allow God to take up the old and lay down the new.

"Adulthood gives each of us the opportunity to be the person that we needed when we were young."[1] So then, how do we *be* the person we needed? Where in the world do I start? Well, it takes work. R.E.A.L work. Not a quick fix, not a pill or cosmetic surgery. Not changing our clothes or the money in our bank account. It takes a complete heart transplant. I needed to let God tear up my old road, with potholes and patches and worn edges, in order for Him to lay down a new road, a new life, and a new heart.

Now that you have made the decision to take the *"One Way"* road, be aware that some of your traveling companions will choose not to follow. Don't be dismayed! You have made the right choice. It may seem that your companions are getting ahead of you, but in reality, they are going around in circles while you are making real progress.

Another thing you must be aware of on the *"One Way"* road is that you will experience *"Road Work Ahead"* that will cause some minor delays or inconveniences on your journey. But this *"Road Work"* is necessary for change and improvement in how you travel through life. No one likes delays, detours, and bumps in the road, but the finished product will be well worth it!

This is the place I found complete brokenness.

How many times have you been driving a road that has a bunch of patches on it? First, you notice the way the patches look. As you drive, it's not smooth. It's quite bumpy and annoying. I find it interesting that these shortcuts are taken to temporarily fill in the potholes. The key word there is temporary. We do that in life as well. We temporarily fill in the gaps or holes, only to leave ourselves like these roads, patched and rough to ride. That was me. Even though I was making progress, and I had made the decision to follow Jesus, I was still a rough road. I was hard to be around. Every two feet, there was some other bump, something else for me to complain about. It was hard to be me. I was frustrated with myself. Others were frustrated with me. I didn't know how to be understood, and I didn't know how to understand other people. To say I was a hot, funky mess was an understatement. Full disclosure—I am still a work in progress. As I continued on, all I could think was, *When does this road get smooth again?* God gently said, "Honey, this road, your heart road, has to be torn up before we can lay down the new. Just think on that for a minute. I'll wait..." All these patches in our lives have to be ripped up, so we can lay down new road.

> "Honey, this road, your heart road, has to be torn up before we can lay down the new."

Because God uses us, He can't have other people traveling our rough roads, getting jostled by our patches and potholes. He needs to lay down new road, which means He's going to have to do some major construction.

Rough Road

I was so moved by the "vision-revelation" that God had given me of His love and concern for me that it fueled me for this next stretch of road on my journey. Though my tank was full of joy, it wasn't long before I hit some major bumps in the road that slowed me down. Nothing runs smoothly down a road that is getting some major reconstruction.

Those bumps were anger and bitterness from past experiences that seemed to surface when confronted with things that triggered my emotions. I remember becoming disappointed in myself when those emotions surfaced, especially after experiencing the glory of God.

We definitely need those glorious times in the Lord in order to be willing to change. I read in 2 Corinthians 3:18, *"But we all, with unveiled face, beholding as in a mirror the glory of the Lord, are being transformed into the same image from glory to glory, just as by the Spirit of the Lord."* This verse says so much that at times it might seem too much to comprehend. But let's look at it more closely so that we can learn what's really necessary for change:

"But we all" means there are no exceptions. If you think you are unworthy, or beyond help, please know that is a lie right from the pit of hell. If you think you are "good enough," that also is a lie. These lies keep us from being all that God would have us to be, which is the very image of his Son Jesus Christ.

"With unveiled face, beholding as in a mirror the glory of the Lord," means when we have a glorious encounter with the Lord, the radiance of Christ is seen on us because we reflect His light to a dark and dismal world. But realize that you cannot wear any masks in His presence. God knows that I have been guilty of wearing masks in order to appear a certain way when all along I was quite the opposite. But that doesn't fly with God! When we look into the face of God through His Word and by His Spirit, it shows us who we are in comparison to who we should be in the Lord. When we humble ourselves and acknowledge our need for His all-sufficient grace and our willingness to change, then there is visible evidence of His glory in us for the world to see.

"Are being transformed into the same image from glory to glory, just as by the Spirit of the Lord," means that each encounter of the glory of God transforms us more into His image. This might sound glorious, but this is where the roadwork (transformation) really begins. What happens in between each experience of God's glory is what makes all the difference in being transformed. This is a work of the Holy Spirit—the very life of Christ that dwells within each person who is born again, which gives us the power to be transformed!

We can read this verse, understand it intellectually, and yet never experience the transformation that it speaks about. Only when we allow God to turn over our way of thinking will our behavior begin to change. Sometimes this can be painful but so necessary for the reconstruction to take place. This is called surrender!

Looking in My Rearview Mirror

Looking back, I can definitely see that a lot of roadwork began in my life after my divorce and confession of my affair. During that season, I was single, and a lot of upheaval took place. Up until that point, I had built my life on a foundation of self-reliance and achievements. I was driven by what I considered to be success in my personal and professional life. God began to take the jackhammer of His Word (Jeremiah 23:29, *"'Is not my word like fire,' declares the Lord, 'and like a hammer that breaks a rock in pieces?'"*) and break up a lot of my thinking as well as the walls that I had built up around myself. After all, who wants to get hurt again? I had built a fortress that prevented me from really letting people in and from me genuinely being able to care about others. It took time to build that wall, and it was going to take time to bring that wall down. Thankfully, God is not in the demolition business. He is a skilled craftsman who knows how to strategically tear down brick by brick and then rebuild on the best foundation.

> It's so much easier to see the roadwork needed in other people's lives than it is to see the work needed in our own life.

Up until this time, my prayer life had consisted of me praying that God would change my circumstances and change the people in my life who were thorns in my flesh. I didn't realize that God's real goal was for me to see that I needed to change. It's so much easier to see the roadwork needed in other people's lives than it is to see the work needed in our own life. Seeing the work needed and being willing to allow God to do the work are two different things. But God has a way of getting our attention!

Being single gave me more time to pursue things outside of my education and career. I got more involved in the church I was attending, where participating in the choir and a community group turned out to be life-changing for me. God taught me how to be vulnerable and to trust again. Seeing other broken people open up honestly to one another taught me that I didn't need to hide behind a mask any longer. Being in community showed me that everyone is broken and needs the healing power of God. I not only heard testimonies of how God changed people in the group, but I was an eyewitness to those changes. To see the tangible proof that God can change a life helped me believe for the change that I so desperately wanted in my own life. There were times I thought, *I'll never change,* but then someone would acknowledge a change they saw in me. That gave me the motivation and belief to continue on this journey, regardless of the roadwork along the way.

One area where I could see change in my life was in regard to receiving correction. At one time, when someone would try to correct me, regardless of how gentle the correction was, I would shut down. I justified my attitude by thinking, *You don't even really know me and now you're trying to tell me how to live my life? I've managed fine without your advice.* But as I grew, when correction came my way (after the initial sting to my flesh), I would ask God for the grace to listen to what was being said and be open to the possibility that they were right. That was a miracle in and of itself. I had witnessed other people in the group accepting correction and that enabled me to be far more receptive myself. But at times it made me feel that there was so much work that needed to be done, and it was taking so much time! Could I really hang in there and keep going, or should I just settle for where I had gotten to on this journey?

Look Out For Potholes

I'm an impatient person and want to see instant results. After all, we live in an "instant" society. Waiting for results causes me to take matters into my own hands or, worse, just give up and settle. But the change that God wants to make in our lives takes *time*. This is where I can get very discouraged and want to throw in the towel.

I began to realize that at times I would act one way at church and another way out of church. Especially when I was home in my "safe place," I compromised on things, like TV shows that I knew were not beneficial to my spiritual growth. But since I was alone, and no one was watching, I sometimes fell back into old behavior patterns, like complaining, gossiping, getting angry and jealous, and the list goes on and on. Those behavior patterns are like potholes that you need to watch for intentionally, or they will give you a flat and derail your journey. Every time I hit one of those potholes, I heard that voice. You know, that *voice* that tells you that you're a complete failure and you will never measure up to be an authentic Christian? That *voice* will condemn you and make you feel hopeless.

But thankfully, God's voice does not condemn. That's how you know the difference. Sure, there are things that the Holy Spirit may convict us of, but conviction and condemnation are two very different things. Condemnation makes you feel hopeless, but conviction shows you how to have hope again. Condemnation is a dead end, but conviction leads you back on the right path.

Condemnation makes you feel hopeless, but conviction shows you how to have hope again.

A Clearing Up Ahead

I questioned if change was really happening. I needed tangible. God did not owe me that, but He knew what I needed. I remember when my community group threw me a party for my 30th birthday. When you leave your twenties and enter the big "3-0," all you can focus on is what you have not accomplished yet. Especially if you're still single and your biological clock is tick-tick-ticking away! There is an undeniable pressure, especially for those of us who are overachievers and feel like we have not achieved very much.

This birthday party turned out to be the very lifeline I needed to keep me from falling into a ditch of despair on the side of the road. I believe God knows how to speak to each of us. My love language is words of affirmation, and God used my community group to give me the affirmation I so desperately needed. Let me set the stage for you. It started with a surprise, and that is hard to get away with. But they managed to surprise me. I was met at our original small group location by only one person. She read me a letter (that I still have to this day), and then escorted me to dinner at my favorite restaurant at the time, Outback Steakhouse! Each woman in my group gave me a card with a word and a description on the back. Each card represented their impression of me. With each card came a rose. They had pre-arranged with the restaurant manager to periodically have the wait staff and patrons come by our table and leave a card and rose. By the end of the night, I had 30 words of encouragement and 30 roses. Almost ten years later, I still have those cards and value them dearly. Here is what they said:

1. *Hard worker:* Characterized by perseverance, Industrious

2. *Achiever:* Prosperous (See: Jeremiah 29:11)

3. *Seeker:* (See: Matthew 6:33)

4. *Genuine:* Not fake or counterfeit, sincerely felt or expressed

5. *Forgiving:* Shows mercy

6. *Support:* Reinforcement, Provider and sustainer, Bearing the weight of

7. *Real:* Having substance, Not taken lightly, Immovable, Reflecting the genuine character of something

8. *Loves God:* (See: Matthew 22:37-39)

9. *Encourager:* Someone who spurs on, Inspires with confidence

10. *Reliable:* Worth of reliance or trust, Authentic

11. *Giving:* Big-hearted, Open-handed with her possessions, her finances, her humor, and her heart

12. *Loyal:* Steadfast in allegiance, True-hearted

13. *Learnable:* A word that describes her character, open to learning more each day about the Lord

14. *Friend:* (See: Proverbs 17:17)

15. *Inspiration:* Guidance, Intuition as part of solving a problem

16. *Strong:* Not faint or feeble, Secure, Of good quality and condition, Spirit and faith (See: Philippians 4:13)

17. *Determined:* Strongly motivated to succeed, Devoting full strength

18. *Wise:* Exercising good judgment or common sense, Discerning and sensible, *having shown experience, knowledge and good judgment*

19. *Intelligent:* Capacity for thought and reason, clever, quick-witted, insightful, discerning.

20. *Vibrant:* Vigorous and active, Kicking butt in her triathlon

21. *Teacher:* Coach, Who she is without even realizing it

22. *Honest:* Marked by truth (See: John 14:6)

23. *Hopeful:* Inspiring when she looks up!

24. *Compassionate:* Sharing in others' sorrow or grief

25. *Perseverance:* Persistent and unyielding, In search of truth, light, and love, Seeking Christ (See: James 1:2-4)

26. *Sister:* Like family (See: Philemon)

27. *Humble:* Not arrogant, Unpretentious, Giving the glory to God.

28. *Energetic:* Industrious, Gumptious, At thirty and more energetic than ever

29. *Captivating:* Capturing interests as if by a spell, The way she expresses her thoughts

30. *Bold:* Fearless, Distinct

For years, the enemy deceived me into believing layers and layers of lies. I was used, unlovable, rejected, damaged, unwanted, adulterer, mistress, murderer, a whore, dirty, isolated, a shame, angry, unforgivable, abandoned, and misunderstood. These 30 words of affirmation have been the new foundation and road the Lord laid down.

Recalculating

So how do we adjust the way we see ourselves? We need to unlearn by learning the truth instead. Diving into God's Word and finding what He says about us is the first place to go. Sometimes we just have to have the words in front of us and read that truth. We look at the internet and take that as truth, yet we don't go to the very truth that God has breathed over us. The following verses were pulled together by Pastor Kevin Blake (EPIC Community Church) to help us outline who we are in Christ and what He says about us. These help us recalibrate our thinking and reset our atlas view of ourselves, through the lens of Jesus Christ.

> *"He has not only laid down this foundation, but it was done wonderfully! (Psalm 139:14) I am made new (2 Cor 5:17). I am forgiven (1 Peter 2:24), washed clean (Isaiah 1:18), delighted in (Zeph 3:17), beloved (Jeremiah 31:3), a sweet aroma (2 Cor 2:15), adopted (Romans 8:15). I am a daughter with a King for a Father (1 John 3:1), a co-heir (Romans 8:17), a temple (1 Cor 6:19), a masterpiece (Ephesians 2:10). I am made whole in Christ (Colossians 2:10), and I am never ever ever ever alone (Deuteronomy 31:8)."*[2]

Some these same themes had appeared on the cards I received on my 30th birthday. It was hard to believe that this was how the group saw me, and I realized that I needed to be able to recognize not only the areas that needed to change but also the work that God was already doing in me. When I hit one of those potholes on my journey, I sometimes pull out those cards to inspire me by the grace of God to live up to the words and descriptions written on them. To God be the glory! Great things He has done and is continuing to do.

PIT STOP PRAYER

Thank You, Abba, Father, Savior, for all the names we can call You. For when we cry out in adoration or for help, we can call upon Your many names, and You hear us. Thank You for hearing us. Lord, some of our cries come from hard lessons we've had to learn. Thank You for the ability to learn the right way. Your way. Please help us make the lessons we've learned habits and a way of life. Help us to exchange our opinions for Your truth so that through the windshield of Your truth, we can see clearly who You are and who we are in You! Guide us around the potholes that try to damage us along the way, and keep us humble so that we receive Your gentle correction. In Jesus' name,
Amen

YOU ARE HERE GUIDE

Under Construction

1. What are some of the names the enemy has tried to call you and lead you to believe about yourself? What does God call you?

2. Do you recognize the need for some roadwork in your life? What will you do to prepare for the work ahead?

3. How do you handle correction? Do you shut down, become
   defensive, or really listen?

4. Have you seen tangible proof in the lives of people around you
   that God is able to change a life? How did that affect your life?

5. What are some of the potholes you keep hitting in your personal life?

6. What inspires you to keep going?

A.R.E.A.

*Finding time and space
to rest in the
midst of the healing.*

hen things are going great and our life is not in upheaval, we can easily forget to take time out to rest. It's important to carve out time and space to soak in what the Lord is doing in and around you. This helps us be in relationship with Him when times are good and bad. When we last set off on our journey, it was in the midst of a storm. It was a tough time in my life and maybe as you've walked through the questions, you worked through tough times you've had in life.

Now that we are looking at these stories through God's view, let's make an area in our hearts for the joy He wants to fill it with. It is so necessary to take time to pull off to the side of the road and get some much-needed filling up so you can heal! They say that an estimated 5,000 casualties on the road are due to fatigue[1]. So often we try to push past the exhaustion that disorients us, impairs our physical senses, and delays our responses. We get so focused on reaching our final destination that we become unaware of what's happening all around us. That includes the blessings the Lord wants to provide.

So let's take some time to pull into one more Rest Area and utilize the power of rest in the midst of healing, before we continue on the last leg of this journey.

A = Alert

Be alert! Sometimes we just go through life, wearing ourselves out, and it puts us in a vulnerable position to be attacked. As God works in you and begins healing areas of your life, the enemy is not going to like it. We need to take time to assess our alertness. Sometimes that means scaling back, assessing our health or schedules, how much we are pushing ourselves, and finding areas where we can cut back in order to really go the long haul. Do you feel under attack? Physically, spiritually, emotionally, maybe financially? Are you alert to what those attacks look like? Take some time to assess where you are and if you're on the right path. If not, this is the time to pray and ask God to show you where to go from here and what to do.

R = Refuel

Being relieved of the weight of the past gives us the opportunity to refuel. There's no greater feeling than the sense of hope for our future that comes when the burden of our past is lifted. It's like a gentle breeze on a hot day. But finding that relief from our guilt and shame requires repentance on our part. All too often, we blame others for our misery. Sometimes our suffering is caused by someone else's actions, but often, with careful reflection, we discover some action or reaction of our own that we need to humbly repent of so that times of refreshing can come to our soul.

> *"Repent, then, and turn to God, so that your sins may be wiped out, that times of refreshing may come from the Lord." (Acts 3:19)*

Applying God's Word to our lives will not only renew our minds but also refresh and refuel our hearts.

> *"The law of the Lord is perfect, refreshing the soul. The statues of the Lord are trustworthy, making wise the simple." (Psalm 19:7)*

So many people go through life running on fumes because they don't take the time to rest. Physical rest offers many benefits that are essential to regaining the strength and stamina necessary to continue on our life journey. But we also need the type of rest that brings peace of mind and willingness of heart to learn from our mistakes and to follow the leading of God. When we repent, God provides His mercy and grace to refresh us, and then He fills us with the Holy Spirit who gives us the fuel to get going! Our dependence on being filled by the Holy Spirit daily gives us real strength and stamina to withstand whatever life throws at us. We need to take time in God's presence each day by reading His Word and praying, asking Him to fill us with the Holy Spirit.

> *"Be very careful, then, how you live — not as unwise but as wise, making the most of every opportunity, because the days are evil. Therefore do not be foolish, but understand what the Lord's will is.*

> *Do not get drunk on wine, which leads to debauchery. Instead, be filled with the Spirit, speaking to one another with psalms, hymns and songs from the Spirit. Sing and make music from your heart to the Lord, always giving thanks to God the Father for everything, in the name of our Lord Jesus Christ." (Ephesians 5:15-20)*

When you are filled with the Spirit, you will be amazed at how different your outlook is regarding the circumstances of your life.

E = Encourage

Often times we are our own worst critic. This negative self-talk can be worse than when others come against us. Now that you have allowed yourself to receive and be refueled, I encourage you to take the time to write words of affirmation and healing to yourself and/or to someone else. This may also be a time to write some healing words of encouragement to your past self.

> *"What, then, shall we say in response to this? If God is for us, who can be against us? (Romans 8:31)*

_____

_____

_____

_____

_____

A = Active

The last step here is to take what we have learned in this time and do something with it. Take an active step toward making a long overdue phone call. Maybe you just need to take time to stop running your schedule into the ground and take a walk right now to just be away from things. Maybe you need to write a letter. Is there a text or card you can send to someone who would be encouraged by your words? Some of my greatest experiences are those that involved actively doing something. Day dreaming and thinking are great, but real life change happens when we put action to our dreams. What can you do today that brings God's Word to life?

"For the word of God is alive and active. Sharper than any double-edged sword, it penetrates even to dividing soul and spirit, joints and marrow; it judges the thoughts and attitudes of the heart." (Hebrews 4:12)

Now that you're well-rested and have taken the time to get refueled and refreshed, it's time to get back on the road as we continue our journey.

MILE MARKER

9

No Passing Zone

*Finding patience and purpose in
blind spots and blockages.*

lright, I'll admit it…I have passed in a no pass zone.
Thank goodness I did not get a ticket or, worse, in
an accident.

You know that feeling in the pit of your stomach that says,
*I really shouldn't do this. Clearly there is a disadvantage here. Someone more
experienced identified this stretch of road as cautionary. But I can do it. Let
me just get around this slowpoke in front of me. Did they not get the memo
that I was coming through today?* Isn't that what we do to God? In
our impatience and arrogance, we send *Him* the memo of our
intended destination and expected time of arrival. *Hey Driver, did
you not get the memo that I am on the road with somewhere to be?*

How often do we do that, though? We hurry others, and we
try to hurry God. Our impatience causes us to miss valuable
lessons in life. And then we wonder sometimes why we go
through the same thing over and over. Because, by golly, God is

God and if He needs us to learn something, He's likely to either keep us in a loop or put something in front of us to slow us down so we can see what He's trying to do in us.

This can be aggravating, am I right? Just like a truck in front of us, we can't see around it. We can't see what's coming up. We can't see how long until the passing zone. We don't know when it might turn off the road and get out of our way. All we know is that we have somewhere to be...like, yesterday.

Can we talk about a little road rage here? I think almost everyone I know has something that ticks them when they're driving. We get hotheaded, anxious, and intolerant. Talk about a joy killer to ourselves and others! Ironically, the other folks that are getting us all riled up usually can't even hear us yelling in our car. But God hears us. If God is slowing you down, pay attention. Sometimes we can miss what is right in front of us because we only have the destination in mind.

How many times have we gotten somewhere and all we have to tell about the journey are the horror stories of traffic and accidents and wrong turns? When was the last time you arrived at your destination and said, "What a great drive!"? Even if you were stuck in two hours of traffic, did you take that time to talk to God, listen to worship music, play car games with family, make a phone call you've been wanting to make? Don't let the enemy take your attention and hold you captive for that time. See the opportunities of how God wants you to use it. Then use it! God is calling you in these moments (or seasons) when you feel stuck behind circumstances out of your control. This is a humbling time, but it can also be refreshing when we use it as God intends.

When you arrive somewhere, do you greet your hosts or friends refreshed and excited? Or are the frustrations of your trip the first things out of your mouth? What about in life? Is your heart full of joy and excitement, or negativity and complaints?

We often come across no passing zones in road work areas. I think it's one of the ways God likes to teach us patience. You know, it's that old adage, "Be careful what you pray for. You just might get it."

I've enjoyed giving patience, when I had plenty to give, but it's not something that I recall enjoying learning. God has shown me how to be more aware of when I need more of it and how to refuel my patience tank faster every time.

So much of our faith journey is an upward climb along a winding road full of blind spots. It is so difficult to see what really lies ahead, and so we must proceed with much caution and patience as we travel along the road set out for us.

The tendency for most people is to rush and pass by much-needed lessons that will equip us for what lies ahead.

When we have come to a place where we are actually allowing God to do some much-needed work in our lives, whether it's letting go of things from the past or old behavior patterns that have been so ingrained in us that we really don't know how to live without them, it will require the grace of God to teach us how to be patient. None of us like to wait. It's probably one of the hardest things to do, especially for the go-getter people like myself, who focus on results and achievements.

When you finally make up your mind to get serious about changing how you live your life and wanting the transformation that the Word of God says is possible, that's when you want to see instant results. I began to approach the change in my life like change management in my career—methodical, transactional, and results-oriented. After all, we do live in an "instant" society with easy access to so many things. But change is not "instant" and it's not "easy." It requires a steadfastness that only God can provide. This is another place in our journey to transformation that requires surrender! We must be willing to travel at the right speed and follow the signs along the road to real change!

Sometimes obstacles get in our way and slow us down, so we think the best thing to do is speed up and pass the very thing that God has intentionally put in our path to produce the patience so necessary for our growth and maturity. After all, patience is a fruit of the Spirit that must be produced and developed in our lives. Even though we see those double yellow lines on this section of the road, we still get tempted to push on the gas and take the risk to pass in the *"No Passing Zone."*

Looking In My Rearview Mirror

I love listening to music. One day, I heard this song by LeAnn Rimes entitled *"What I Cannot Change."* I really can relate to the lyrics of this song. She talks about our comforts and wanting our own way, our impatience and need for instant gratification. Yet she exposes a humility in the song as she talks about the awareness of our weaknesses and our dependence on God to pray we won't make the same mistakes. One of the lines that really hit me hard was when she sings about our pain being self-inflicted. You see, our impatience is self-inflicted.

These lyrics really hit a chord in my heart, summing up exactly how I was feeling. The song made me recognize that while we cannot change things from our past, we *can* change how they affect us in our lives today. I realized the change that was necessary in my life was my own responsibility. Yes, we can ask people to pray for us, and that is very biblical, but at the end of the day, we need to pray for our own transformation and ask God to give us the grace and mercy to move from a wounded heart to a wonder-filled heart, a heart filled with God's amazing grace.

Women especially tend to use most of our energy caring for the needs of others, primarily because we are so concerned with how others perceive us. Most of us are driven by our need to be needed. So we spend very little time on the self-care that can bring healing and health to our emotions and, more importantly, to our spiritual life.

Most of us are driven by our need to be needed.

Those old hurts can be like a slow-moving tractor-trailer in front of us that we just want to pass regardless of the risk. But sometimes it requires recognizing and acknowledging the hurt before it will get out of our way. There's nothing more freeing than when that tractor-trailer finally turns off the road and we have clear passage at last. If we had ignored those double yellow lines and allowed our impatience to get the best of us, who knows what would have resulted—possibly more hurt or, worse, a spiritual casualty.

An Obstacle on My Road to Transformation

I had just finished Beth Moore's *Breaking Free* Bible study, and I was ready to do the work necessary to put my past behind me and get moving. This was a good season in my life. I was feeling a spiritual awakening, and my relationship with the Lord had never been more real to me. In addition, I had met Brent and was engaged and soon to be married. Everything seemed good when, out of nowhere, I started to experience some real health issues. Over time, I had developed endometriosis, Graves Disease, and a goiter that had become very noticeable. Instead of moving ahead with my life, I had major setbacks physically and emotionally, which eventually affected my spiritual growth. For over a year, I had one doctor's appointment after another, with every scan imaginable. At one point, they thought I had thyroid cancer, so I was sent to a specialist, an endocrinologist, who turned out to be the worst doctor I had ever been to in my life. After some time, I finally found a good doctor who was able to give me a proper diagnosis. He performed surgery to remove my thyroid, and it seemed like everything would be getting better. But after the removal of my thyroid gland, I gained an exorbitant amount of weight because it took some time to get stabilized on my medication. All of this started to affect my performance at work. It became hard to focus, and though I knew the information needed to get my job done, I felt like I was in a mental fog. I found myself getting angry and frustrated because nothing seemed to be getting better. My weight just continued to escalate. No matter what I tried, nothing seemed to help me get it under control. It just seemed like it was taking forever for things to get better. This was my tractor-trailer that was totally in my way and preventing me from moving ahead, and there was no way around it.

> God doesn't set us up for failure. But He does put us through times of testing.

All the setbacks that I was experiencing seemed to bring out the worst in me. I began to see those old ugly attitudes that I thought I had dealt with and surrendered to God. I used all the energy I could muster to keep them under control at work, but the people closest to me got the brunt of my anger and frustration. This only led me to become discouraged and disappointed, especially since I had thought I was making some real headway in my spiritual growth. I started to get angry with God, feeling like He had let me down. I felt like I was set up to fall back into my old way of thinking and acting, even though I knew in the depth of my heart that God doesn't set us up for failure. But He does put us through times of testing.

Picking Up Momentum

Discouragement brings us to a fork in the road. We can give in to "this is the way my life is always going to be," or we can start believing God for a change to take place. Some things only God can do, but then there are action steps we need to take in order to work along with God's answer to our prayer for change.

I came across an article about bariatric surgery and started talking to my doctors about it. Individually, those doctors probably would have never made that recommendation to me, but when I started talking to all of them and they started consulting with each other, the option became a reality for me. I went to Franklin Square Med-Star program and, six months later, had a gastric sleeve laparoscopic surgery. Recovering from such an extensive surgery can be overwhelming, both emotionally and physically. Anyone going through the surgery must be monitored for about five years to make sure there are no complications. In addition, you start out on only a liquid diet, then transition into baby food, and it takes months before you're able to eat solid food. Talk about the need to be patient! I really didn't have any other choice since my body was now calling the shots. But regardless of the food restraints, I was moving and making progress once again and began to see some results. The weight loss motivated me to press through all the other obstacles.

Of course, life doesn't just stop happening when you're going through health issues. There are still family problems, issues at work, and situations with friends that can all add to the stress you're already going through. Stress can really hinder the recovery process after surgery if you don't learn to rest mentally, emotionally, and physically.

But I really think this is all part of the test. You know, the *big test*—the testing of our faith. Academically, I do very well on tests, but in the past, I didn't have the same track record with the testing of my faith. How we handle stress is a major indicator of who has the control—you or God! I've learned that far too many things are beyond my ability to control, so when I find myself stressing, I just stop and pray. Sometimes the lyrics of songs like "Jesus Take the Wheel" or "What I Cannot Change" come to my mind, and even though they are helpful to refocus my thinking, they don't have the power to *change* my thinking. But God's Word has the power to transform us by the renewing of our minds.

> *"Do not conform to the pattern of this world, but be transformed by the renewing of your mind. Then you will be able to test and approve what God's will is – his good, pleasing and perfect will."* (Romans 12:2)

Recalculating

Being impatient is easy. It's the natural reaction. So how do we change that natural instinct into a response that is more easygoing? How do we delight in the waiting and slowing down process?

If we just move over and go past something without the due diligence of the experience, what will we miss?

> **How we handle stress is a major indicator of who has the control—you or God!**

It's a counterproductive move. The fear of missing out causes you to *actually* miss out on the experience you were meant to have. When we can't see what's ahead, how do we get to a place of not worrying about what's to come and enjoying what we have before us? We may not realize it in the moment, but these times of forced patience are usually something we actually have prayed for. In the movie *Evan Almighty*, Morgan Freeman plays God, and talks to Evan's wife in a scene:

> *"Let me ask you something. If someone asks for patience, you think God gives them patience? Or does He give them the opportunity to be patient? If he prayed for courage, does God give him courage, or does He give him opportunities to be courageous?"*[1]

He goes on, but the point is that we have to look at the situation for what God is doing in it. Not what we want it to be. This is the place we lean into when we ask why something is happening. It's an opportunity. Don't ask, "Why, God?" Ask, "What, God? What do You want me to learn, and where do I need to grow in this time of waiting?" You see, there are times when we are speeding along, things are great, and we are in the zone. But there will be times for us to slow down, stop, reassess, prune, and grow in areas that God wants to use. Ask yourself when you are impatient, is God bringing something to light? Do you need to slow down, prune back, and recalculate your direction and speed?

During stressful times, it's important to spend quality time investing in your relationship with the Lord. Instead of becoming frustrated with that tractor-trailer slowing you down, ask the Lord to show you what He wants to teach you through the experience. Whether it's a health issue, a financial problem, relational difficulties, or family concerns, just to name a few, they are all tractor-trailers that we cannot pass by. Instead, as we travel more slowly, we can be open to learning how to turn the problem into a life-changing purpose.

Hindsight is always 20/20. You don't see what God is doing in the moment, but when the road finally opens up and you are able to pick up some momentum on the open road again, you can see the things you have learned in the "*No Passing Zone.*" For me, it was a time of learning how to let go of trying to control everything around me and, as a result, becoming more giving and forgiving. Of course, these lessons are often ongoing as we travel along on our faith journey and God continues to refine us. The lessons come with a price, but the price is so worth it! Finding joy in knowing that God is working is priceless!

This was a time in my life that I truly learned to see the Lord and trust Him to take control of my life. Isaiah 6:1 states, "*In the year that King Uzziah died, I saw the Lord seated on a throne, high and exalted, and the train of his robe filled the temple.*" Some earthly "kings" had ruled my life for so long, and they needed to die in order for me to truly see the Lord in His rightful place in my life. In all of our lives, some old things need to be removed so that we can not only see the Lord but be filled with awe and wonder as we behold His majestic presence in our lives. We are His Temple, and He desires to fill us with passion, power, and purpose!

As important as going to church, reading your Bible, and praying are to your spiritual growth, nothing is more beneficial than learning to trust God in midst of the trial in the *"No Passing Zone"* so that we can arrive...happily.

PIT STOP PRAYER

Lord, You are the epitome of patience. Your wrath is real, yet You withhold from us with divine understanding of our need for grace. You make the earth turn at the perfectly designed speed. You are the Creator of all space and time. Your timing is perfect. If our lives are busy, chaotic, and going at a pace faster than we can keep up, it is likely due to our own doing and not Yours. Lord, please help us see our need to slow down. Help us not react but rather respond. In times of delay on our speedway, help us find joy. Support our desire for discernment on what we cannot change and be clear about our role in what we can. When we cannot change what has been placed before us, give us peace and serenity to know Your presence. Thank You that You love us so much even when we are living busy and hurried lives. Lord, we lift up our impatience in exchange for Your peace. In Jesus' name, Amen.

YOU ARE HERE GUIDE

Are We There Yet?

1. Have there been any tractor-trailers in your life that have slowed you down? Explain.

_____

_____

_____

_____

_____

_____

_____

2. How do you react when there's a slow-moving vehicle in front of you in a "*No Passing Zone?*"

_____

_____

_____

_____

3. Is there something in your life that you realize you cannot change? How has that affected you?

4. Can you describe a trial from your life that taught you some valuable lesson(s)?

5. Write out a scripture that has made a lasting impact on your thinking.

MILE MARKER

10

Merge / Yield

Learning to yield to others' needs and developing a submissive heart.

I ecided to put these two signs together because they both seem to apply to one of the most important areas of our lives: relationships. Learning how to be in healthy relationships is vital to our emotional and spiritual growth. Whether it's learning to be a brother, sister, daughter, son, parent, or true friend, or learning to have an intimate relationship with someone of the opposite sex, it requires a willingness to "*Yield*" the right of way to another person in order to "*Merge*" your lives together and travel in the same lane.

Of course, one of the major differences between family relationships and friendships is you cannot pick your family, but you can pick the people you decide to do life with. Our initial exposure to relating to others begins at home with our family. Regardless of our family dynamics, we learn to relate to others within our family structure. Our family life reinforces our strengths, weaknesses, fears, and insecurities.

The fact that our family life shapes how we relate to others might, in and of itself, seem cause for despair if your upbringing was anything like mine. Thankfully, when we put our trust in the Lord Jesus Christ and enter into a relationship with Him, He teaches us how to do life with others. The Word of God and the Holy Spirit teach us how to relate to people with love, compassion, mercy, and His all-sufficient grace. There is such a vast difference between religion and a relationship with Christ! Religion restricts, while a relationship with Christ releases. Instead of rules and restrictions, we are free to establish healthy boundaries in our relationships with others. It is essential to allow the Holy Spirit to guide us through life and set up those guardrails (boundaries) in all of our relationships.

Religion restricts, while a relationship with Christ releases.

Think with me for moment. You're driving, and you're coming up to a *"Merge."* What happens? For the merge to work smoothly, there must be yielding and acceptance. One car has to slow down and allow the other to come into the space in front of it, submitting to the other car's need. The other car has to accept the offering of the person providing that opening. How many times have you been the car trying to get in and no one wants to create space for you? How frustrating, right? I know I find myself yelling out the words on the sign, "Alternate, people, alternate!"

Why do people become so selfish over one car length? Similarly, why do we behave so selfishly when it comes to the needs of others? The sacrifice is usually not that large. God is not asking us to make big sacrifices all the time. He's not asking us to give up our entire car. He just asks for a car-length spot that will help someone else. Overall, He's asking us to submit our selfishness. Even though it may seem like a sacrifice, we actually get the greater benefit when we learn to submit. For those who take the open spot, a little (nice) hand gesture, blink of the lights, or some small signal of thanks goes a long way. And think about that, too, when someone else lets you merge. They have submitted to your need. Let yourself receive that gift of someone else's submission.

In this process of merging and yielding to God, to His desire and what He is asking of us, we also have to accept those openings when He provides them. He invites us to join in, to be part of the main flow of things. He wants you to feel like you belong and you are accepted through the submission of His Son Jesus Christ.

Looking In My Rearview Mirror

Growing up, I was definitely "Daddy's little girl." I was very close to my father and not close to my mother, but that has totally flip-flopped over the years. Now as an adult, I can see how unhealthy my parents' relationship with each other was. My father's obsession with my mother not only caused them to divorce three times from each other, but it created an emotional "divorce" between my father and me. He never seemed interested in what was going on in my life. He would just use our time together to try to pry information out of me about my mom. I know that he loved and cared for his children, but he never fought to have a relationship with us. He just couldn't control the obsession he had with my mother for so many years.

When I was single in my mid-twenties, he came to my house one time to help lay some floors. We got into a huge argument about my mother, and he literally got in my face. He said he would take down anyone who tried to get in his way between him and my mom.

Those words made me feel I was not his daughter but merely someone who was in his way. After he left the next day, I didn't speak to him for five or six years because I was so hurt. The fact that he saw me as a barrier to what he wanted rather than his daughter made me realize we really had no relationship. I also realized I needed to set up some boundaries so that I would not be continually pulled into the drama of my parents' relationship. My dad's fixation caused him to miss walking me down the aisle when I got married, seeing his granddaughter born, and being a part of my family life.

I can't heal my dad. I can't fix him. All I can do is set healthy boundaries so that I can grow as a person. I love him and respect him as my father and have prayed for him, but I had to release my hurt and pain and wait on the Lord to bring some real stability in my dad and in our relationship. The Lord has been faithful! A couple of years ago, my father did come to meet his granddaughter and spend some time with my husband and me. He seemed to be able to stay within the boundary line and only brought up my mother once or twice over four days, which really was a miracle.

Setting boundary lines takes courage and confidence, especially for people who want to please others. Dr. Henry Cloud and Dr. John Townsend state,

"Having clear boundaries is essential to a healthy, balanced lifestyle. A boundary is a personal property line that marks those things for which we are responsible. In other words, boundaries define who we are and who we are not. Boundaries impact all areas of our lives:

Physical boundaries help us determine who may touch us and under what circumstances.

Mental boundaries give us the freedom to have our own thoughts and opinions.

Emotional boundaries help us to deal with our own emotions and disengage from the harmful, manipulative emotions of others.

Spiritual boundaries help us to distinguish God's will from our own and gives us renewed awe for our Creator.

Often, Christians focus so much on being loving and unselfish that they forget their own limits and limitations."[1]

I truly had to understand and set my limits in regard to my relationship with my parents. That realization has spilled over into other relationships in my life. Over those five or six years of being single, I spent a lot of my time getting educated, not only academically but also emotionally and spiritually. I wanted to learn how to be a healthy person so that when I had children, they would be healthy. I remember reading the *Five Love Languages for Singles,* and that was the beginning of learning how to be in healthy relationships with people. After all, we all need to learn how to be a good friend before ever being a good spouse to someone.

All too often, the dysfunction we grow up with becomes normal to us. But because God is not only love but also light, He begins to shed light on those dark areas in our thinking and emotions. We begin to recognize His peace and that exposes all the chaos that we were once accustomed to. Looking back on my first marriage, I realize that dysfunction was my normal, but

I didn't want to live like that any longer. I knew there were things that I needed to change in order to avoid the same mistakes I had made in the past. I wanted to be open to what God desired for my life, but that would take willingness on my part. I had to learn to be open and vulnerable with God before I could ever be open and vulnerable with people.

Learning to Yield and Merge

Prior to meeting my now-husband, I had been dating someone on and off for a few months. He had all the best intentions, but whenever he told me he loved me, I would think, *How can you love me? You don't even really know me. You only know what I've led you to believe about myself.* Then I realized that I felt the same way about God. I thought I loved Him, but I really didn't know Him well enough. I think I had an appreciation for God and a respect for the authority of God, but I could not love Him until I got to know Him and His love for me. This was a big wake up call for me. I realized the only way I could truly learn to love was by first knowing God's love for me. The Bible states in 1 John 4:19, *"We love because he first loved us."* Until we know God's love for us, it's impossible to truly love another person. We might be infatuated with and attracted to someone, but that is not really love. Really knowing God's love makes you secure enough to be open and transparent with others, and to allow other people to know the real you. It also teaches you how to appreciate people for who they are, not merely what they can do for you. If we are honest with ourselves, many of our friendships are probably based on

> Setting boundary lines takes courage and confidence.

what that person provides for us. Once they no longer provide anything valuable to us, we have no real use for them. I know that sounds heartless, but think about it. How many really intimate friendships do you have? Oh, you might know a lot of people, but that does not make for an intimate friendship. Intimate friendships acknowledge the good, bad, and ugly parts of the person and are willing to work through the dark places together. Intimate friendships are honest, sincere, and sacrificial, but they also have realistic expectations of the other person.

When you are open to learning how to have healthy relationships, God is faithful to send someone into your life who will be willing to learn along with you. I remember when I met my husband, Brent. I knew that this was no ordinary relationship. In the past, my relationships always started off on level two or three, where I was attracted to them, and quickly skyrocketed to level ten. Before long, the relationship would drop down, kind of like a mudslide. We would hit a peak, only to spend the rest of the time trying to save the relationship and get the momentum back. It was like trying to build on sinking sand. But with Brent it was different. It continued to grow each day, and every conversation just got better than the one before. Instead of building on sand, it felt like we were building on a firm foundation.

I remember talking about my relationship with Brent in my community group and sharing how it felt like we never hit the high point because each day it got better. Looking back over the past eight years together, I can honestly say I look forward to each new day together. Of course, we have our differences, and we can rub each other the wrong way, but thankfully, we have learned to agree to disagree on a few things and ultimately come to common ground so we can work together.

Being connected to my local church and community group taught me a lot about myself and how to be a more giving person, which included my time, talents, and treasures. When I met Brent, it was like putting all that I had learned from God's Word to the test. But the test proved easier than I had expected because Brent was very real about who he was, including his weaknesses, and that made it easier for me to be transparent myself. I knew that God was changing me, because in the past I had imagined my husband would be someone in a prestigious career. Yes, I openly admit that my prejudice and feeble-minded, media-clouded misconceptions played a huge role in that desire. But Brent was a blue-collar worker, and it really didn't matter to me. I just fell in love with his heart and the fact that, right out of the gate, he was so real that it allowed me to let down my self-protecting guards that I had lived with for so long. I finally felt the confidence to really let him into the most personal parts of my heart. At one point, I thought if he really knew all the things I had done in the past he would run to the hills, but even when I told him what happened in previous relationships, Brent never judged me. He embraced me. He embraced all of my rearview stories and experiences and understood that it was about the heart. I had a desire and drive to change, and I invited him into my crazy car for the ride that has become our marriage and our life together! His acceptance of me just as I was made me love him all the more and value the relationship so much that I didn't want to do anything to jeopardize it.

Recalculating

Remember in a previous chapter I shared about the consequences of my affair? Well, for a short period of time our working relationship still overlapped, and I needed to contact him for information required during an application process for a new position that was offered to me. In congratulations, he sent a ridiculously huge bouquet of flowers to my house. When Brent came over to my house, he asked me who sent the flowers. I hesitated—and I lied to him. I said I liked them so much I got them for myself. Lying to him made me want to throw up. It was definitely the old me taking over, but I was afraid to tell him the truth. I didn't know how he would react, and I really liked him a lot. But I couldn't live with myself. Up to that point, I had been so open and transparent with him. So later that night, I drove to his house, which was a good distance away, just to confess to him, hoping he would forgive me. I told him that I lied about buying the flowers for myself and that they were sent to me as a congratulatory gesture from *him*.

When you yield the right-of-way for someone else, it is a sign of trust and respect.

At first, Brent was upset, but then he said he understood where I was coming from because of the newness of the relationship. I confessed to him because I really wanted this to be a long-term relationship that would hopefully lead to marriage and a family. I didn't want to build it on a foundation of lies, because you know one lie turns into another lie and so on and so on. When I got home from his house, I threw the flowers away, and I told him that I would never lie to him again. I wanted our relationship to be built on trust and respect.

You see, when you yield the right-of-way for someone else, it is a sign of trust and respect. You're allowing that other person to make the next necessary move so you can merge together and travel in the same direction. When I went to Brent and confessed my lie, I was yielding to him—more evidence of the change that God was doing in my life. I wasn't allowing bad habits to ruin this relationship that was important to me. Even admitting the relationship *was* important was a sign that God's grace was at work in my life, and the remorse I felt when I lied to Brent was the sweet conviction that I pray will always be present in my life. Allowing God into the most private places of my heart to reveal some of my deepest insecurities has made me much more secure. Today, Brent and I are happily married, and we have a beautiful daughter, Nacelle.

This area of yielding and merging doesn't only apply to romantic relationships. It also applies to friendship. At one point, my best friend, Keri, and I were growing apart, mainly because of the differences in our lifestyles. She was married and had her first child while I was still single and had absolutely no concept of the demands of parenthood. She wrote me an email stating that she felt our friendship was no longer going anywhere and felt it was necessary to pull back. I was dumbfounded. I cried for days. But the Lord revealed to me that I was being a bad friend. He asked me, "How much does she mean to you?" I knew our friendship was worth fighting for. It was one of the relationships that are truly worth yielding to so that you can merge on the same lane of life. Some relationships are temporary and come and go, but there are others you cannot imagine doing *life* without. For the relationship to continue on a healthy path, you must be willing to take ownership for your part of the problem. I had gotten lazy in my relationship with Keri, forgetting birthdays, being insensitive to her new role as a mom, and neglecting other things that make for a good friendship. I wasn't willing to let her "divorce" me, and I knew I would need to be sensitive to her needs and submit my selfishness. I asked the Lord to reveal to me the areas of my heart that needed recalculating and requested forgiveness from my dear friend.

All of this plays out in the most important relationship of all—our relationship with the Lord. Learning to yield to His leading in our life is vital for us to travel on the path that He has laid out for each of us. Whether you're married or single, to grow emotionally and spiritually you must yield to God's Word and the guidance of the Holy Spirit.

> *"Now then,' said Joshua, 'Throw away the foreign gods that are among you and yield your hearts to the Lord, the God of Israel.'"*
> *(Joshua 24:23)*

PIT STOP PRAYER

God, You are the head and author of family.
Your design for family is perfect. We are family
through and in You. Our earthly family dynamics shape how
we engage in relationships. Thank You for the gift of relationship.
Through connection with people, we are able to find our strengths and
weaknesses and learn to grow into our purpose. Lord, help us heal
from past hurts that allow fear and insecurity to keep a hold on us and
that impact the development and growth of our relationships. Help us
honestly evaluate who we have around us and establish healthy
boundaries. We lift up the minds and hearts of those who need help
setting boundaries. Please provide Your gift of discernment and clarity
on the health and status of our current relationships. Help us to
be wise, kind, caring, and helpful as we connect with
people where they are so that You are at the
center of our community. In Jesus' name,
Amen.

Guardrails and Passengers

1. Can you recognize any family dynamics that have shaped your relationships as an adult?

2. List a strength, a weakness, a fear, and an insecurity that still affect your relationships.

3. Are there any present relationships in which you need to set up boundaries? Explain.

4. How can you establish the necessary boundaries? What steps do you need to take?

_____

_____

5. How can you better connect with people to establish intimate relationships?

_____

_____

_____

_____

_____

_____

_____

6. Describe in your own words the importance of yielding for the purpose of merging your life with others.

_____

_____

_____

_____

_____

_____

_____

_____

MILE MARKER

11

Detour

Preparation for divine destiny is in the redirect.

With great anticipation, we can proceed, looking forward to all that life holds for us. We might expect to get to our destination without any delays, but how many of us know that is not reality? You can be traveling along at a relatively good pace when, all of a sudden, you come across a "*Detour*" sign that not only delays you but also brings you down some unexpected roads. Life has a way of throwing a monkey wrench into your plans that can cause you to get frustrated. You just don't have time for this!

Hopefully, we have gained some much-needed wisdom on this road trip so instead of getting frustrated, we begin to look at the detour as an opportunity to display all we have learned and the progress we've made thus far. There is a big difference between reaction and response. In the past, we might have had a knee-jerk reaction, but now we have the understanding to make a wise response. All we have experienced thus far should have given us a new perspective when something unexpected causes a delay in our plans. Instead of being frustrated, we can intentionally look for God's purpose!

Sometimes, we need to be thankful for those unexpected things in our life. There are a few verses in Alanis Morissette's song "Thank You" that relate to this very concept. A series of thank you's take you off guard at first as she thanks frailty, disillusionment, terror, consequence, and silence.

When I first listened to the song, I thought, *Why would anyone be thankful for those things?* My young and inexperienced mind just liked the artist and her bold lyrics. In the same section of the song, she displays the wisdom she has now from those experiences and is thankful for them. Now that I have a different, wiser perspective, this was the first song that came to mind when I thought of learning to be appreciative through detours. When you come out the other side and see the purpose for them, you can't help but be thankful instead of resentful.

Looking In My Rearview Mirror

In a previous chapter, I talked about my health issues and the bariatric surgery that I had undergone. The recovery process was extensive, and it required me to be on short-term disability for at least six weeks. I made the necessary plans for the strict regimen I would need to follow for those six weeks, and I was looking forward to getting my life back on track. I envisioned my "hot new body" and wanted to do everything necessary to accomplish my goal. After the surgery, it's very difficult to eat anything. You start out with only liquids, but then you have to work up to soft food to get an adequate amount of protein. I was worried, because there can be serious health issues if your protein levels drop too low. In addition to getting the nutrients needed for recovery, it was equally important to get physical rest and minimize the stress in my life. One particular day, I was having trouble keeping anything down and I decided to call the nurse for advice. She mentioned the importance of keeping my stress level down in order for my stomach to properly process the food I was taking in. I was determined to follow her advice. Then, less than half an hour after hanging up with the nurse, I received a call from my brother telling me that my mother had suffered a stroke.

Within a couple of hours, Brent and I jumped in the car and drove from Maryland to Tennessee. So much for lowering my stress level! Sometimes you just have to do what you have to do! Most of us women can totally relate to that concept.

It was ironic that we had planned on going to Tennessee the following month to move my mom to Maryland. She was in the process of packing when all this happened. We had made the arrangements to move her into a townhouse, but now all those plans were out the window. Keep in mind that this was only ten days after my surgery, and I had not fully recuperated.

When we got to Tennessee, Mom was mostly paralyzed and had a stent coming out of the top of her head to relieve the pressure of fluid on her brain. Initially, everyone swarmed to the hospital, but after a few days, I was the only one able to stay with her because I had time off from work (because of my own recovery). Looking back on it all now, I can see how God used this detour in my life to show the change that had taken place in my own heart. In the past, I would have been totally frustrated, but I sensed a grace on me that enabled me to put everything into the right perspective. I was learning to look to God in my circumstances rather than looking to myself, because He is *bigger* than any of our problems.

> *"The Lord is my rock, my fortress and my deliverer; My God is my rock, in whom I take refuge, my shield and the horn of my salvation, my stronghold." (Psalm 18:2)*

Turning Point

All of this happened during a time when I was experiencing a lot of new things. Brent and I were celebrating our first wedding anniversary, plus I had just started a new job and had surgery that would be life-changing. Everything I had planned for this time was put on hold and pushed to the back burner, so to speak. I started my new job in May, then I had the surgery in July, and right after that my mom had her stroke, so it completely changed the trajectory of my career path with this new company. It was very humbling to accept their willingness to work with me since they barely knew me. But I knew that it obviously was God's favor and grace, and it was a turning point in the way I chose how to handle this detour.

Sometimes you can see God's favor even in small things.

I began to realize and accept that I was not in control, but rather God was in control of all the events in my life. Sometimes we can see God's favor even in small things.

While my mother was in the hospital, she had to eat soft food, and when her doctors found out that I recently had bariatric surgery, they provided me with the same diet. It was a little thing, but it was something my mother and I were able to share.

Over the seven to eight weeks that she was in the hospital, we witnessed one miracle after another. She had to get a full craniotomy where they opened up her skull and removed a tumor in her brain stem, the motherboard of the entire body. The nurse at the hospital said 95% of the people who came to that Neuro Trauma Unit didn't leave alive. Wow, that's pretty intense! The tumor was encapsulated, totally round, so they were able to remove it entirely. The chances of something like that are extremely slim. Each day was a new and difficult challenge. Left to myself, I probably would have been exasperated. But in the morning, I would spend time in prayer, asking God to give me the love, compassion, grace, and strength necessary to really be there and be present for her. It took two months to get her to the point where she could be moved and discharged. That alone was a miracle.

On a more personal note, another miracle worth mentioning was how much my mother really appreciated me being there for her. During that time, two events passed: my one-year anniversary with Brent and my birthday. I couldn't afford flying home for both, so I decided I would fly home for two days to celebrate my anniversary and then stay in Tennessee for my birthday. My mom, while completely helpless, had two nurses go to the hospital bakery and get me a cupcake and a candle. It made me cry. She just wanted to tell me how much she appreciated me being there and how proud of me she was. In *her* own mess and recovery, she showed me how to care for others. She cared for me in that moment. Even though she could barely lift her arms, she insisted, with the nurses' help, that *she* hold the cupcake and hand it to me. I guess stubbornness runs in the family! This might seem like a little thing, but it was the beginning of God bringing real healing to our relationship.

"He heals the brokenhearted and binds up their wounds." (Psalm 147:3)

Recalculating - Seeing Purpose in the Detour

We were finally able to move Mom from Tennessee to Maryland, where she was admitted into a nursing home. During her stay there, she developed an infection and was admitted into the hospital, which became our ticket to get her home. I would not have been able to get her out of the nursing home directly. In the meantime, I was trying to get back on track at my new job and was driving seventy miles to the hospital from work and seventy miles back home. We eventually hired a private full-time nurse to care for her. All of this took a toll on me, but not like it might have in the past. Something was different, and that something was me!

Prior to my mother's stroke, we had planned on her moving to Maryland so that she would be close to Brent and me. She found a townhouse she fell in love with, and it was an opportunity for us to build a new relationship as adults. I had never really had a close relationship with my mother, mainly because of the dysfunctional relationship she had with my father. I was looking forward to this being a season of change in our family. I can see now that instead of us trying to build a relationship on a rocky foundation, God was stripping us both down for the purpose of building us up on His firm foundation of love and respect. Up to this point, my main focus had been on what I wanted and needed, but this unexpected detour put my focus on my mother's needs and gave me the opportunity to become her caregiver. I remember that while in the hospital, my mom's feet got very encrusted with dry, dead skin because she wasn't doing any walking. So one day I asked the nurse for gloves and a basin. For four hours, I washed and peeled away layers and layers of skin that had accumulated on her feet, and I cried. It felt like I was also peeling away layers and layers of old hurts, past arguments, and years and years of decay. As I peeled the decay from her feet, the Lord peeled layers of decay and callous from my heart, giving me the will to face and tackle any obstacle that came my way.

All during this time that I was caring for my mom, I was still going through my own physical recovery and had to let Brent and my in-laws care for me so I would have the strength to care for my mother. I began to realize that God was going after the very same thing in both my mother and me—*pride,* which is grounded in self-reliance. My mother was in diapers and needed someone to change and bathe her. My needs were very different, but it was still humbling to really need others to care for me, both physically and emotionally. I lived with constant concern for my mom's wellbeing, and it weighed heavily on me. I found myself crying all the time, out of exhaustion but also out of appreciation for the care I was receiving so that I could care for her. Every day, I became more and more aware that my strength comes from the Lord!

"My help comes from the Lord, the Maker of heaven and earth."
(Psalm 121:2)

On top of all this, we also had the financial concern of all the medical bills, which were astronomical. When Mom retired, she didn't maintain her health insurance, so she had no coverage.

Between the medical care, medicine, ambulances, two helicopter transports, and nursing care, her medical bills totaled $650,000. I went through all her old insurance paperwork looking for a glimmer of hope, but it seemed nothing would give, until another miracle occurred. Low and behold, one day the insurance company finally said that if I paid the previous two months of premiums, her health insurance would be reinstated!

This whole experience helped me see my mother through different eyes. I had always viewed my mom as a victim, but now I was beginning to see her as a fighter. Her being in my care was an opportunity to really put the past behind us and start building a new relationship. This was the season of change that I had been praying for, and it took this *"Detour"* to my plans to get us on the right road!

PIT STOP PRAYER

Dear Heavenly Father, we believe in Your purposes for our lives. Your divine design sometimes requires us to be redirected. Those redirects and detours sometimes take longer than we prefer. Help us rest in Your divine will. Give us peace when the fear of the unknown takes over our peace. When we have uncertainty in timing, help us to be certain of You. When it's difficult to let go of our plan for ourselves, we lift up our resentments and ask that You help us relinquish control and allow You to take us down Your designed path. As we traverse that path, we ask that You bring us healing and prepare us for what is ahead. Heal our broken hearts from the loss of our desires and prepare us to accept Your will for our lives. Bring us overwhelming joy in that acceptance. Sometimes these diverted dreams will cost us the price of lost relationships, jobs, money, etc. We praise You for the gain of blessing, spiritual growth, joy, and never losing hope in You. Thank You for Your Word and the scriptures to keep in our hearts and minds to remind us and rely on when we need that peace for the longer road that we are on.

YOU ARE HERE GUIDE

A Place of Healing

1. Can you recall a time you had to take a major detour in your life?
   Explain.

   _____

   _____

   _____

   _____

   _____

   _____

   _____

2. Looking back, can you now see the purpose for that detour?

   _____

   _____

   _____

   _____

   _____

184

3. What road did the detour take you down, and how did you handle it?

4. What did this detour cost you? What signs of healing were evident in you?

_____

_____

_____

_____

_____

_____

5. What verse(s) from the Bible really helped you let God come in
   and take control?

_____

_____

_____

_____

_____

_____

_____

_____

_____

_____

_____

_____

MILE MARKER

12

Exit

Healthy transitions from endings in life to new beginnings.

$\mathcal{S}$ olomon said, "The end of a matter is better than its beginning, and patience is better than pride" *(Ecclesiastes 7:8).* I *think one* of the greatest lessons in life is to know *when* to end something. All through life there will be *necessary endings* that require us to have the courage and the wisdom to end something so we can begin something new. The *"Exit"* of one thing is really the beginning of something else. Please note, it is important to know how to transition out of one thing before proceeding into *new beginnings.* You definitely don't want to take old baggage with you into the new leg of the journey. Whether it's a relationship, a divorce, a career choice, a job, or even an old way of thinking, the transition process is essential for change. Remember, *change* requires *us* to change.

"Considering that we have to deal with endings all of our lives, most of us handle them poorly because we misunderstand them. We tend to either take endings too seriously, confusing them with finality, or we fail to take them seriously enough. They scare us, so we try to avoid them."[1] But the longer you avoid ending something, the longer it prolongs the problem you need to resolve in your life. You will never really appreciate the new beginnings that God brings your way unless you leave behind the old. That doesn't mean that you have no memories or "souvenirs" of those past events in your life. It merely means you don't allow the past to hinder the future. Even hurtful things from our past can have a positive impact on our present and future if we learn the valuable lessons they provide.

One of the greatest lessons in life is to know *when* to end something.

Exits may seem final, but there is only one final exit from this life. I recently heard a young man, named Jake, say on a social media Goalcast video, "None of us get out of life alive." In his graduation speech—a time of transition for him—he reminded his audience that life is finite. We will go through many transitions in our lives. The exits and endings in our life are not the finality. They are just transitions to new beginnings. They end a phase, but without endings, there can be no new beginnings.

Looking In My Rearview Mirror

The purpose of looking back is only to remember where we were and where we are going. There is a reason rearview mirrors are small, while windshields are wide and large. God doesn't want us to linger in the past, but to take what we've learned in the past and bring it forward with purpose. Take that glimpse into the rearview mirror of your life with a fresh perspective so that when you glance back, you can leave the negative behind and focus on the truth and the wisdom that God wants to bring into your future.

Through my profession, I helped write hundreds of resumes. I found it interesting how often people sold themselves short with their experiences. Once I had the chance to sit down and talk with them about their past experience, my fresh perspective translated their experience into skills, knowledge, talents, and qualifications that they never saw as valuable. From then on, they saw themselves differently, and it influenced their future job applications and even the way they carried themselves. They were able to look back and see the value of their experience through a different lens.

Where they believed they lacked experience, the revision gave them a new forward-looking view. It opened their eyes. It cleaned their windshield so they could see the future through the lens of a revised perspective of their past.

The portion of scripture that comes to mind is where Paul exhorts us to *"forget what is behind and strain toward what is ahead"* (Philippians 3:13).

He doesn't mean to act like it never happened. The word *forget* does not mean to never think of the former things. Rather, he means not to live in past failures or successes. All of our failures are under the blood of Jesus. Once we repent, God never holds them against us, so we should not hold onto them. Paul also knew that no matter what successes we've accomplished in our life of faith, there will still be more to apprehend. We should never plateau and think that's all there is for our life.

> God doesn't want us to linger in the past, but to take what we've learned and bring it forward with purpose.

When we hold onto the negative aspects of our story, we allow that hurt to hold us hostage. We may think we have moved on, but in reality, we've just moved on to the next day and brought the hurt and pain with us. When we do this over and over again, at some point we become so weighed down with offenses, grudges, and unforgiveness that it keeps us from moving forward or upward at the speed the Lord wants us to. He's over there trying to get us to speed up, and here we are with boots on our tires (that we insist will stay until the person who offended us takes them off). Look, sometimes the Lord does slow us down, but sometimes we let our own insecurities and past hurts keep us from moving forward faster. We don't like the uncomfortable-ness of new things, even when new is better. The safest place for us is in our own heads and hearts. Even when our heads and hearts are filled with junk, it feels safe to us. This is why hoarders don't leave. They know they have a problem, but anything new to them is too foreign and scary. It's easier to stay in the comfort of the misery we know than move to the unfamiliar of the happiness we desire.

We need to stop hoarding our hurts and let the cleanup crew in to get rid of it all. We have to let others in to help. That means starting something new and working to envision what that new thing looks like.

Progressing into new beginnings requires us to *"strain toward what is ahead,"* which means we need to be intentional not to allow old ways of thinking into our new way of living. Paul never settled or allowed himself to plateau, but rather, *"I press on toward the goal to win the prize for which God has called me heavenward in Christ Jesus"* (Philippians 3:14).

As believers in Jesus Christ, it is vital to our spiritual wellbeing to recognize our God-given purpose in life. That purpose, regardless of the logistics, is to represent Christ here on earth. We are far more interested in *walking on water* and achieving great exploits than learning to *walk on dry ground*. Walking on dry ground produces the character that represents Christ to a hurting, dying world. People want to see authenticity and longevity, not the razzle-dazzle that is so prevalent in Christian culture today!

With that being said, we need to recognize the *necessary endings* in our life. We need to intentionally press forward and not allow certain relationships or circumstances to keep us lifeless. That doesn't mean that everything in your life needs to end. There are many good things in life that continue to add to our growth, development, and happiness. Ongoing relationships or things in your life may take different shape over time. Knowing how to work through the changes of those phases and their small endings and beginnings will make those relationships and circumstances stronger for the long haul. But some things are simply not good for us and cause us to become unproductive and unfulfilled. As we grow in our faith, we need to also become *"confident and comfortable in seeing, negotiating, and even celebrating some endings that will become an open door to a brighter future."*[2]

I remember when I felt that God had impregnated me with the message for this book. I knew it would require some logistical changes in my job, home life, and finances. I would have to be intentional about making the adjustments necessary to accomplish what God had put on my heart to do. The prospect was exciting, but it would take real wisdom and courage to put an end to the way my life had been and enter into a new season. Of course, there is never any guarantee of what the future holds, but unless we have the courage to take the steps forward, we will never discover the potential of new beginnings. There is always a personal cost involved in ending what you have known in order to enter into the unknown, but when you're able to look back for a moment and see the faithfulness of God, even when you were not faithful, it minimizes the fear associated with those necessary endings.

"She is clothed with strength and dignity, and she laughs without fear of the future." (Proverbs 31:25)

A New Perspective

As Christians, we know that there is an ultimate destination for us. We have not "arrived" to that final destination of spending eternity with the Lord, but in our day-to-day life experiences, we are *"getting there"* with the little victories we make along the way. Learning to let the Lord guide us in and out of the roads of life is where we experience real peace, joy, and fulfillment.

"You hold me by my right hand. You guide me with your counsel, and afterward receive me to glory. Whom have I in heaven but You? And there is none upon the earth that I desire besides You. My flesh and my heart fail; but God is the strength of my heart and my portion forever." (Psalm 73:23-26)

When we truly believe that God is in control and we allow Him to guide us, we will be amazed at where He leads us. It might not always be easy, but the final outcome will be well worth the price of trusting Him all the way. Of course, a lot of the realization of all this is hindsight. You never really see what God is doing while you're smack in the middle of some episode in life. Take my divorce, for instance. While going through it, I felt disconnected from any possibility of a happy and healthy relationship in my future. I never could have imagined at the time that I would meet a man like Brent and my entire life would be changed for the better. A lot happened between my divorce from Andy and my marriage to Brent, and it required me to reorient my thinking, choices, and feelings. During those six years, I couldn't allow myself to be controlled by my emotions, or lack thereof. I had to learn to trust in the only One who sees the outcome and allow Him to guide me though all the potholes, detours, and every other mishap on this road called *life*. Even when we are going through the middle and our feelings are off the chart or, worse, non-existent, it's important to intentionally remember that this is not all there is! But it will take time, effort, and skill to get from *where you are* to *where you are going*. It doesn't happen overnight!

Learning To Follow New Road Signs

With experience comes a measure of understanding, but experience alone will not change the trajectory of your life choices. Added to experience, there must be a willingness to follow the guidelines found the in the Word of God along with the promptings of the Holy Spirit. The very first commandment Jesus gave to His disciples was, "Follow me." If we are honest with ourselves, most of us tell Jesus, "No. You follow me and bless me!" That is like us getting in the car and telling the GPS to create the way as you drive it. Letting God plot our course is the very first change that must take

Letting God plot our course is the very first change that must take place for us to be well-prepared.

place for us to be well-prepared on the road of life. This means exiting and ending our old lives and old way of thinking. Exiting the life that is familiar. Even if life lacked hope and joy, it's what we've grown accustomed to, and we stay where it's comfortable. I love a quote from the movie, *The Greatest Showman*, "Comfort… the enemy of progress."[3] We sometimes have to get uncomfortable to make progress.

That means you may feel pain or experience disappointments, but they won't have the damaging effect on you they had in the past. You'll begin to almost laugh as they happen. I know that sounds crazy, but that is why I love the "she laughs" in Proverbs 31:25. I chuckle now when adversity comes my way. The enemy tries the same old tricks on the new person that I am becoming. I appreciate the tests now. They give me confirmation of what I hope and pray are the transformations within me. When the Holy Spirit and I take them on with ease, it brings faith to life. If you never felt pain, you would never enjoy the times of peace and joy.

The first and most important "*necessary ending*" is when you stop trying to lead your own life and humbly accept the help and guidance provided for you. Without taking the "*Exit*" from "*Self-Reliance*" and getting onto the road entitled "*God Reliance*," you will find yourself making the same mistakes and going around in circles most of your life. The amazing thing about *salvation* is that the rest of our life is not about trying to fix ourselves or fix the mistakes we've made. Our salvation means we've been given *rebirth*, a fresh start where the past is no longer an issue and going forward is our big new beginning.

We will continue to go through transitions in life, and they will be uncomfortable. Let's journey gently, as we all fall short. None of us are "there." As William Bridges says in *Transitions*, "It's time to be gentle with yourself or with the other person, a time for the little supports and indulgences that make things easier. I'm not quite fully the new person yet, but I'm getting there."[14]

PIT STOP PRAYER

Lord, You are the Alpha and Omega, the beginning and the end. You are the ultimate Author of all beginnings and all endings. You have designed our days to have beginnings and ending cycles, to remind us not to be afraid. We do not have to be afraid to start or stop anything in life. Because You provide fresh mercies for every new thing. Hours, days, weeks, months, and seasons are all made to remind us it is never too late to start fresh and to give us peace to know we may leave the "thing" behind. Lord, we ask for Your wisdom and knowledge to recognize necessary endings and to help us to forgive. Forgiveness releases us so that we may embed Your truth in the space of our hearts and minds where resentment once burrowed. Give us wisdom through the forgiveness and healing process to fuel the long journey of serving and honoring You with our lives. We ask that You help us embrace that all endings are new beginnings. In Jesus' name, Amen.

YOU ARE HERE GUIDE

New Beginnings

1. What necessary ending are you presently having to face? Are you afraid of it? Why?

2. Just ending something does not necessarily change the course of your life. Something in you also needs to come to an end (change). What change within yourself do you now recognize is necessary?

3. How will that change play out in your day-to-day life?

4. Do you have a problem with forgive and forget? What does God say in His Word about it?

5. What do you need to do to change your perspective on necessary endings?

Road-trip Remix
(Songs and Psalms for Getting There)

Dear Friend, "Music is the moral law. It gives soul to the universe, wings to the mind, flight to the imagination and charm and gaiety to life and to everything[1]" (Plato). It is no surprise that the Psalms are songs of music for our souls. There isn't a Psalm that does not breathe life for our bleeding souls. I hope and pray that you find these selected Psalms and songs for you on your journey comforting and life-giving as you continue to travel through the broken road. Thanks, Linette

12 Psalms for the Road

1. Psalms 31:7
2. Psalm 30:1-3
3. Psalm 9:1-2
4. Psalm 24:5
5. Psalm 32:3-7
6. Psalm 46:5
7. Psalm 51:13-17
8. Psalm 63
9. Psalm 62:5
10. Psalm 84:10
11. Psalm 119:67-68
12. Psalm 139:1-4, 23

12 Songs for *Getting There* Playlist

1. "What I Cannot Change" – LeAnn Rimes
2. "Who You Say I Am" – Hillsong
3. "Jesus, Take the Wheel" – Carrie Underwood
4. "Here" – Kari Jobe
5. "Different" – Micah Tyler
6. "Turn Around" – Matt Maher
7. "Bless the Broken Road" – Rascal Flatts
8. "I Got Saved" – Selah
9. "I Surrender" – Hillsong
10. "Even If" – Mercy Me
11. "Break Every Chain" – Tasha Cobbs
12. "Fix You" – Coldplay

Notes - Billboards

Introduction: Roadside Assistance

1. *Facebook*, s.v. "Tony Robbins," accessed March 5, 2017, https://www.facebook.com/TonyRobbins/posts/most-people-have-a-dirt-road-to-happiness-and-a-highway-to-pain-condition-yourse/10155157902079060.

Quote

1. *Brainy Quotes*, s.v. "Bob Marley," accessed September 13, 2018, https://www.brainyquote.com/quotes/bob_marley_167100.

Mile Marker 1: Enter

1. Wenburg, Andrea. "Your Mess Can Become Your Message – Megan Swanson." *Voice of Influence.* Podcast audio, June 16, 2017, http://andreajoywenburg.com/your-mess-can-become-your-message.

Mile Marker 2: No Outlet

1. Dr. Seuss, *Oh, the Places You'll Go!* (New York, NY: Random House, 1990).

Mile Marker 3: Winding Road

1. *Wikipedia*, s.v. "Serenity Prayer," accessed August 27, 2017, https://en.wikipedia.org/wiki/Serenity_Prayer.

Mile Marker 4: Wrong Way – Do Not Enter

1. Dr. Seuss, *Oh, the Places You'll Go!* (New York, NY: Random House, 1990).

2. *Betterhelp.com*, s.v. "Seven stages of grief," accessed August 4, 2018, https://www.betterhelp.com/advice/grief/understanding-the-stages-of-grief.

3. Renee Fisher, *Forgiving Others, Forgiving Me: Finding Freedom in the Journey from Pain to Purpose,* (Eugene, OR: Harvest House Publishers, 2012), 97.

4. David Wilkerson, "Pride and the Voice of the Spirit," DavidWilkersonToday.blogspot.com (blog), September 14, 2018, http://davidwilkersontoday.blogspot.com/2009/08/pride-and-voice-of-spirit.html.

5. Suzanne Tucker, *Toolkit Manual 2.0,* (St. Louis, MO: Generation Mindful, 2018), 27.

Mile Marker 5: Dead End

1. Cole, Lynn. 2017. "He helps us persevere past our problems..." Facebook, September 11, 2017. https://www.facebook.com/groups/riseupwriterscommunity/permalink/1556972517657515/?comment_id=1557137304307703&reply_comment_id=1971026346252128&notif_id=1536944047954667&notif_t=group_comment_mention.

Mile Marker 6: U-Turn

1. Jane Garee, "Jane Garee: You're Not Wrong, You're Recalculating," MaryCravets.com (blog), March 6, 2018, https://marycravets.com/2016/06/27/jane-garee-youre-not-wrong-youre-recalculating.

Mile Marker 8: Road Work Ahead

1. Suzanne Tucker, *Toolkit Manual 2.0,* (St. Louis, MO: Generation Mindful, 2018), 8.

2. Kevin Blake, "My Identity in Jesus" (Handout received at Epic Community Church, Aberdeen, Maryland, January 3, 2017.

Rest Area 2 – A.R.E.A.

1. National Highway Traffic Administration, "Drowsy Driving: Asleep at the Wheel," CDC.gov (blog), August 6, 2018, https://www.cdc.gov/features/dsdrowsydriving/index.html.

Mile Marker 9: No Passing Zone

1. *Evan Almighty.* Directed by Tom Shadyac. Hollywood: Universal Pictures and Spyglass Entertainment, 2007.

Mile Marker 10: Merge/Yield

1. Henry Cloud and John Townsend, *Boundaries Updated and Expanded Edition,* (Grand Rapids, MI: Zondervan, 2017), Back Cover.

Mile Marker #12: Exit

1. William Bridges, *Transitions: Making Sense of Life's Changes, Revised 25th Anniversary Edition,* (Cambridge, MA: De Capo Press, 2004), 107.

2. Dr. Henry Cloud, *Necessary Endings: The Employees, Businesses, and Relationships That All of Us Have to Give Up in Order to Move Forward,* (New York, NY: HarperBusiness, 2011), 9.

3. *The Greatest Showman.* Directed by Michael Gracey. Hollywood: Twentieth Century Fox, Chernin Entertainment and TSG Entertainment, 2017.

4. William Bridges, *Transitions: Making Sense of Life's Changes, Revised 25th Anniversary Edition,* (Cambridge, MA: De Capo Press, 2004), 173.

Songs for Getting There

1. Brainy Quotes, s.v. "Plato," accessed September 11, 2018, https://www.brainyquote.com/quotes/plato_109438.

Acknowledgments – Bumper Stickers

"God has given each of you some special abilities;
be sure to use them to help each other, passing on
to others God's many kinds of blessings."
(1 Peter 4:10a, TLB)

One of the best pieces of advice I've received was, when you get where you are going, reach back and help someone else *get there.*

I would like to thank the people who have helped me *get there...*

First and above all, I come humbly before the Lord. Thank You for Your love, grace, forgiveness, and Spirit. It is only through the power of the Holy Spirit that I am able to boldly share the message of Your power of healing, transformation, joy, and abundance in the fullness of God. Thank You for revelation and creativity. Thank You for gently redirecting my ways, back to You, time and time again.

My husband, Brent! You always support me in whatever comes our way, be it through my crazy dreams or through the circumstances beyond our control. Your willingness to go raw and real in the depths of our brokenness challenges me. Thank you for taking this leap with me and loving all of me and my rearview! (LOL).

To my dearest daughter, Nacelle. You gave me such great memories in my writing space and sacrificed mommy time so I could finish this project. Thank you for scribbling all over my writing board and sharing your stories through drawings. Your creative mind inspires me to infinity. I pray that with the Lord's guidance, Daddy and I help guide you along your own road toward a life full of hope, love, and endless joy. Thank you for the hugs and bringing Mommy tissues when I cried tears into these pages.

Keri Smith—I love you. Period. You know I am writing these words through tear-filled eyes! I can't even thank you without crying from adoration for our relationship. You're my flashlight! Thank you and Jeremy for being on this road trip with me, and for the bonfire that made these chapters come to life. You always share my enthusiasm for analogies. Thank you for your endless love, laughter till it hurts, and for demonstrating Christ's love to and with me.

Valerie Moreno! A piece of my heart is forever in Texas because of you! We are truly heart sisters. My heart aches when we are apart. Your passion for family has healed deep wounds in my life. You have ridden in this proverbial life car with me (and even down the wrong way, literally). I love all of our adventures, and I am eternally grateful for the gift the Lord brought to me in you!

To my mothers-in-law, Sherri Stevenson and Donna Bumford. Thank you for your support, encouragement, and your last-minute availability for childcare with my new schedule. Because of you, time was made available in the craziness of life to write these words. It takes a village to raise a child, and it also takes one to write a book. Thank you for being my village always!

To Andrea Wenburg—This project actually got off the ground because of your passion for giving the heart words to speak. Because you followed your calling, I finally put words and action to mine. I finally released and melted the fear that kept my words frozen. Thank you for your core message teaching from the start. Your transformation markers set the stage and brought inspiration for my "mile markers." It brought clarity to my chaos of thoughts, and you taught me how to embrace the Power! Your passion for bringing voice to the heart is impeccable. Your superpower is your Voice of Influence! (http://www.voiceofinfluence.net/)

To my book baby doula and coach, Renee Fisher. You have been there to labor with me through this message delivery. You are relentless with encouragement! Your uplifting coaching through every stage, every step, every emotion, and every phase of the creative process is downright magical. You gave me a safe place to create freely, think vastly, ask all the questions, express all the feels, and allow God to truly breathe into my life through this process. You were my AAA when I ran out of fuel. THANK YOU! (#allcaps)

To my writing support, Michele Amodio. I love what the Lord has done by bringing us together. He did what we prayed for from the start. He wove our hearts together to bring this message of His love and grace to others. Thank you for your time, your talent, your wisdom, your creativeness, your friendship, and the freedom to agree and disagree in a godly way. You supported me through this experience and taught me even more wisdom about my experiences along the way. Thank you for translating my heart into words.

Rebekah Benham – thank you for your editing, proofreading, and honest and constructive feedback. Thank you for caring for the reader and message as much as I do. Your talent, support, and encouragement was a great boost in my fuel tank during the final stretch. You are seriously gifted!

Encouragement Warriors: EPIC Community Church Ladies Group, thank you for your encouragement through all of the seasons this project has taken. You have been there from the beginning! Your unending prayers through this project's speed bumps and your eagerness for me to finish kept this project going even when the enemy tried to veer me off the road. Thank you for all your feedback and anticipation for this story of God's redemptive power. Thank you for your passion to study God's Word.

Frontline (McLean Bible Church) 2005-2009 Small Group. Your willing hearts gave me a safe place to be vulnerable with every aspect of my dark places. The foundation of our relationships set the standard for how I do "life together" and relationships for the rest of my life. Thank you Ronnie, Jennifer, Jesse, Karissa, Kristin, Victoria, Jodi, and Elizabeth.

To my Total Praise Choir Crew: Daniele, Wes, Amanda, Nate, Evonne, Jess, and Brian! You guys are forever a part of my beating heart!

To my professional family at work! Your "yes" to my request to "change lanes" allowed me to say yes to this longing in my heart. Thank you for giving me flexibility and freedom to express my struggles, and for supporting my personal dream without sacrificing my professional one.

Mom, you are so brave. Braver than you give yourself credit for. Thank you for supporting me in sharing our stories. May our continued journey of healing, continue to be a blessing to others as we share the power of God's healing through the daily healing between us. I love you!

Dad, you have your ways! Thank you for teaching me hard work, setting goals, and to NEVER QUIT! Love you!

A special thank you to Jeddy (Mrs. Jesse Black)! You shared a dream with me. You thought I would think you were bonkers, but you shared the dream with me with such passion and conviction, I knew God was using you to speak this into existence. That dream rocked me to the core, and I never, ever forgot what you shared with me. Thank you for your faithfulness and obedience! You specifically shared with me a vision of driving along a road. You saw signs, and in that dream, I was sharing words and encouragement to many while they held a book that I wrote! Well, here it is! Thank you, my dearest stinker! ☺ I miss your face!

Thank you, *Getting There* launch team! Your feedback, commitment, and support helped the book take a few more turns to amplify the message. You helped this book *Get There!*

The stories in this book are my honest, subjective perception and reflection of what I experienced. I relied heavily upon my own memories and journals of the moments in my life. I verified with the people involved when possible. In other instances, I omitted names.

This book has been a journey within a journey. It has breathed fresh spirit into my life. Everything we do has the opportunity to point us to life or death. To you, my fellow traveler, I pray that your path leads you to life everlasting. I am grateful for your gift of attention. I pray that you find hope, courage, and inspiration in sharing my adventure to *Getting There!*

> **Thank you for traveling with me!**
> **Praying for your continued journey!**
> **God Bless!**

About the Author

Linette Bumford is a Jesus-follower, wife, mother, and author. She is an ambitious, focused, and determined thought leader. A USAF veteran and MBA graduate, she is a trusted advisor and mentor in her profession. Linette drives creative excellence, confidence, and high-quality standards in every aspect of her personal and professional life. She is passionate about inspiring others to fulfill their wildest dreams, achieve their goals, and live vibrantly, boldly, and confidently. Her favorite mantras are "Do the Hard Things" and "All that Jazz." Linette lives in Maryland with her husband, Brent, daughter, Nacelle, and their dog, Titan.

Connect at LinetteBumford.com

Linette@LinetteBumford.com

96510040R10121

Made in the USA
Middletown, DE
31 October 2018